A REVISED EDITION

TROY

WITH LEGENDS,
FACTS,
AND NEW DEVELOPMENTS

ORIGINALLY WRITTEN IN ENGLISH

BY

MUSTAFA AŞKIN
PROFESSIONAL GUIDE

WRITTEN BY : Mustafa AŞKIN
TRANSLATION : Mustafa AŞKIN
PHOTOS BY : Ahmet ESİN, Hans PAYSAN
GRAPHIS BY : Gülten GENÇ
RECONSTRUCTION AND COVER : Semra AKBULUT
COLOUR SEPERATION : Şan Grafik
TYPE SET : Deniz ÇIRA
PUBLISHED AND PRINTED : Keskin Color Kartpostalcılık Ltd. Şti. Matbaası
DISTRIBUTED : Keskin Color Kartpostalcılık San. ve Paz. A.Ş.
Ankara Cad. No.98 34410 SİRKECİ - İSTANBUL
Tel : 0 (212) 514 17 47 - 514 17 48 - 514 17 49 Fax: 512 09 64
BRANCH OFFICE : Kışla Mah. 54. Sk. Günaydın Apt. No: 6/B 07040 ANTALYA
Tel: 0 (242) 247 15 41 - 247 16 11 Fax: 247 16 11

ISBN 975-7559-37-7

CONTENTS

FOREWORD TO SECOND EDITION

The present book is a revised and enlarged edition of " THE GUIDE BOOK OF TROY" which was first published in English and in German in 1981. The book created great interest and was admired by many visitors. With the help of my fellow guides it was later published in French, Italian and Dutch. But the results of new excavations and research have made some parts of the book out of date. Revising the book became necessary. Despite the extensive additions this second edition has almost the same highly regarded layout. I have included in this book all the information and interesting things about Troy that I have learned since the first book was published. As I was writing, my aim was to make you love even the smallest piece of stone at Troy as much as I do.

Some guide books to Turkey describe Troy as "a pile of rubble" or "not worth seeing." It is true that the most significant things were taken away and because of unsystematic excavations many important buildings were destroyed. The local people used Troy as a stone quarry for a long time. But even so, if you have a good guide, you too will be fascinated by Troy, you too will love it.

As most visitors are not interested in archaeological details, I have endeavoured to write what most people would like to know about Troy. Besides this, as an official guide who was born and grew up near Troy, I guide tourists several times a day in different languages. Visitors ask so many interesting questions. In this book, I have especially tried to answer the most frequently asked questions.

The book deals as before with the discovery of Troy in the nineteenth century, the excavations, the different cultural strata and the legends and facts about Troy. It also provides information about the surrounding area and new developments. As well as giving the visitor all the information he needs for a rewarding tour of the site, I hope I have produced a book which can be read with pleasure both before and after a visit to Troy.

MUSTAFA AŞKIN

ACKNOWLEDGEMENT

I am grateful to Hamit Kartal, my dear teacher and the first director of Troy, for making scores of important suggestions for the book and for infusing in me his love of Troy from his boundless experience. I also thank him for protecting and looking after the ruins of Troy during the twenty years of his directorate. I am also grateful to Prof. Manfred Korfmann, the leader of the new excavation team which has been working at Troy since 1988, for kindly inviting me on the tours he organises for the team at the end of every season.

In addition I would like to thank Prof. Charles Brian Rose, the chief classical archaeologist of the team, for his explanations and for allowing me to read his own articles.

THE TROJAN FAMILY TREE

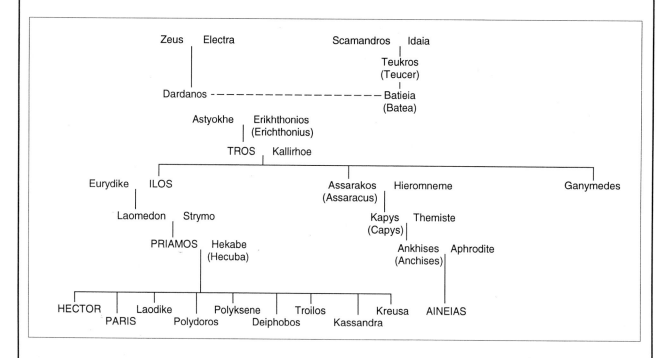

THE NAME AND LOCATION

The lands between the Dardanelles, Sea of Marmara and Edremit Bay were called "TROAS" or "TROAD" in ancient times. Archaeologists discovered many ancient sites in this particular corner of Asia Minor. The most important of all is Troy which probably either took its name from the area or gave its name to the region. It may well be possible that this well-known ancient settlement mentioned in the Iliad as "TROIA", "ILION" or "ILIOS" took these names from the two kings, TROS and ILOS.

It seems that a new discussion is going to give a new name to this most famous city. An article written by Colin Campbell in "The New York Times" on 28 th January 1985, created much excitement, telling as it does how Prof. Calvert Watkins, a Harvard linguist, discovered the existence of another epic poem written in an Anatolian language 500 years before Homer, beginning "When they came from steep Wilusa..."

Prof. Watkins believed that this was the opening line of a song or epic about Troy which was written down in "Luvian", an ancient language spoken by the Trojans. "Steep Wilusa" is the "Steep Ilios" of Homer's Iliad. This interesting theory was argued at a symposium held at Bryn Mawr college in October 1984 in the USA. You will read more about this subject later in the book.

DISCOVERY AND EXCAVATIONS

Troy was accepted as a legendary city for ages. Not many people believed in the existence of Troy. But the location of Troy is clearly depicted in the Iliad with the word "Hellespont", the ancient name for the Dardanelles, and "Mount Ida", the highest mountain of the Troad which is called Kaz Dağ (Goose Mountain) today. Zeus, father of the immortals, used to watch the Trojan war from the peak of Mount Ida.

"The willing pair flew off on a course midway between the earth and starry sky, and brought him to Gargarus, a peak of Ida of the many springs, the mother of wild beasts, where he has a precinct and a fragrant altar. There the father of men and gods pulled up his horses, freed them from the yoke, and wrapped them in a dense mist. Then he sat down on the heights, exulting in his glory and looking out over the Trojan city and the Achaean ships."

The Iliad VIII. 45-51

The rivers Scamander and Simois are the two famous rivers mentioned in the Iliad. The Scamander, todays Black Menderes, arises from Mount Ida, meanders through the Troad and meets the Simois in front of Troy, running together to the Dardanelles across the flat plain where the Trojan War took place. According to legend, the meeting spot of the two rivers is the place where Athena and Hera met to plan the destruction of Troy.

"There, at the watersmeet of Simois and Scamander, the whitearmed goddess Here stopped her horses and released them from the yoke. She hid them in a mist, and Simois made ambrosia spring up for them to eat. Then the two goddesses set out on foot, strutting like pigeons in their eagerness to bring help to the Argive arms"
The Iliad V. 774-779

Legend mentions the islands of Tenedos and Imbros. They are the nearest islands to Troy. By adding the description of "Steep Ilion" and "windy Troy" we describe Hisarlık Hill where the ruins are.
Today at a distance of 30 km from Çanakkale towards İzmir the ruins of Troy can be visited. Standing on a hill at Hisarlık and looking southeast

you can see the summit of Mount Ida in clear weather. When you turn towards the Dardanelles, you will recognise the Scamander and Simois rivers, like two green ribbons of trees down on the plain. As you are standing on the ancient hill top looking out over the famous plain of Troy where once the Trojan War took place, if you are blessed with a little imagination you can easily feel the excitement of the Trojan War, while the famous cool north wind blows from the Dardanelles.

HOW TO VISIT TROY

First of all, the best way to visit this most complicated site is to go with a guide. It is always possible to find some guides near the ruins, especially in summer, includind the author of this book. If you want to walk alone you can easily follow the plan in this book. Though the plan looks deceptively flat and simple, for I have especially endeavoured to use

only the visible or partly visible parts of Wilhelm Dörpfeld's plan to make it simple and understandable, the site is very complicated, so that a person could find one foot in one age and the other foot in another. Having this general idea before you start, buy your ticket and follow the road over the lower town through the roses and you come to the parking area where the wooden horse stands. The road behind the horse will lead you directly to the ruins. Walking under a century old oak tree, and after climbing a few steps at the end of the road, you face the ruins. On the right side you see the monumental city walls of Troy VI and a tower. Before you walk down the steps towards the walls, examine them from a distance. If you climb the steps on the right you will get a birds eye view of the walls and other ruins. When you are looking at these walls imagine that 3000 years before our time King Priam and his people used these walls to defend their city againts the Greeks during the Trojan War. This tower and the walls are the eastern unit of the fortification.

The Eastern Wall of Troy VI

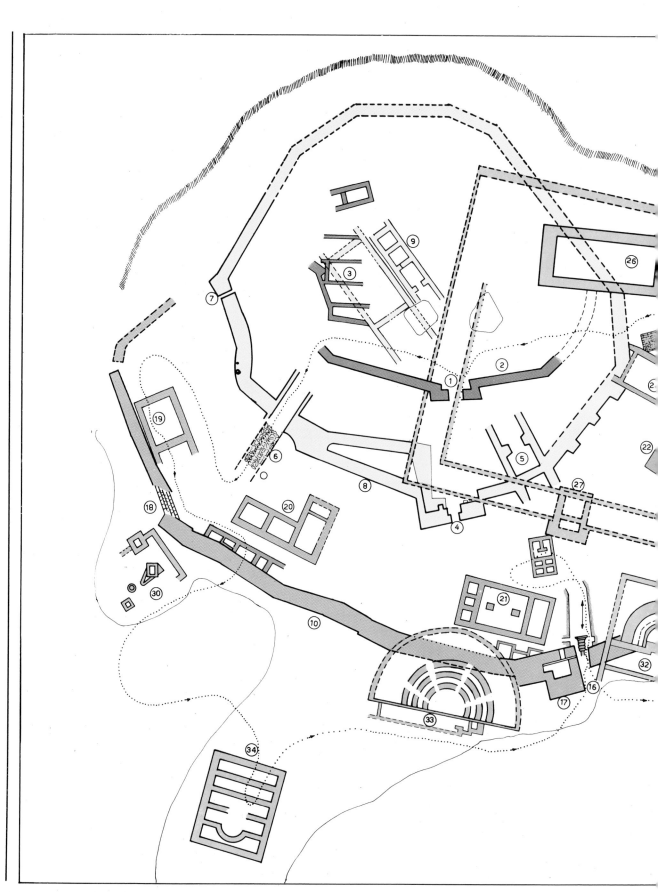

PLAN OF TROY

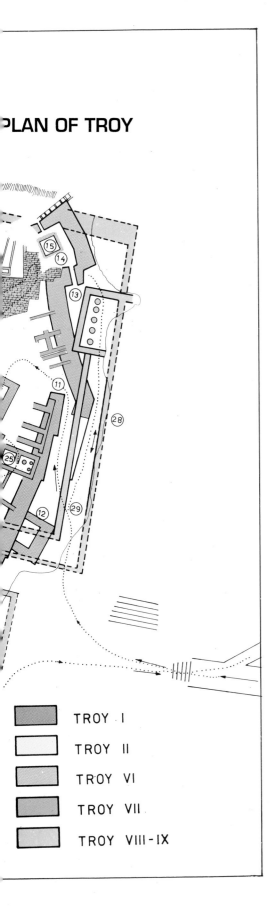

TROY I

TROY II

TROY VI

TROY VII

TROY VIII - IX

1- GATE

2- CITY WALL

3- MEGARONS

4- FN GATE

5- FO GATE

6- FM GATE AND RAMP

7- FJ GATE

8- CITY WALL

9- MEGARONS

10- CITY WALL

11- VI. S GATE

12- VI. H TOWER

13- VI. R GATE

14- VI. G TOWER

15- WELL-CISTERN

16- VI. T DARDANOS GATE

17- VI. I TOWER

18- VI. U GATE

19- VI. A HOUSE

20- VI. M PALACE - STORAGE HOUSE

21- PILLAR HOUSE

22- VI. F HOUSE WITH COLUMNS

23- VI. C HOUSE

24- VI. E HOUSE

25- VII. STORAGE

26- ATHENA TEMP

27- ENTRANCE TO THE TEMPLE (PROPILAION)

28- OUTER COURT WALL

29- INNER COURT WALL

30- HOLY PLACE

31- WATER WORK

32- PARLIAMENT

33- ODEON

34- ROMAN BATH

The South-Eastern Tower of Troy VI

Walk down the steps to have a closer look at the impressive remains of this brilliant and famous period. While you are walking by this wall, compare it with the one on your right, and note the difference in quality, The wall on your right is the outer court wall (temenos) of the Temple of Athena from Roman times. The inside of this wall was filled with soil to make a platform to build the temple. The reason why these almost 3500 year old walls are so well preserved is that they were under the platform of this temple for ages.

At the end of these sloping and segmented city walls of Troy VI and VIIa, you come to a corridor gate. The east gate was cleverly constructed, between overlapping walls. Here the inner court wall of the Temple of Athena cuts the overlapping wall of the east gate. While entering the city through the east gate note the thickness of the fortification wall and especially the stone foundations on both sides of the gap. Imagine that once there was a wooden door closing the space between these walls. This door could not be seen from outside and could not be destroyed by a battering ram, for there was not enough room to manouvre.

After passing through the gate climb the steps. You come to a house from Troy VI on the left side. If you walk to the left from the corner of this house, you will see an interesting house with 12 stone bases for wooden pillars, five on both east and west, and two large ones in the center. This interesting house was possibly used in both Troy VI and Troy VIIa as a temple. In the beginning it had one floor and the door was on the southwest. You can also easily observe the fireplace in the southwest corner just by this old door. Afterwards a second storey was added to the building and the door was moved to the west. Note that this west door is higher than the old one; note also the holes on the west wall were once the wooden beams were placed.

In between this house and the city wall, a house with storage

Eastern Gate Troy VI

vessels can be seen. The wall of this small house were made of unworked stones, rough but thick and strong. This is a typical house from Troy VIIa. Compare this house with the handsome houses of Troy VI. Troy VI houses were large and well constructed, but the houses of Troy VIIa were smaller, almost all of them had storage jars beneath the floors and the structure of these houses was simple and rough. The city did not have a plan. The Trojans built these houses wherever they found a platform, whether on the streets or by the city walls. This can only be explained as preparations for a siege. That is, the people who lived normally outside of the city walls came in when the war started. This is why, without paying attention to building constructions well, just to squeeze everyone in, they built small houses everywhere. Also during excavations arrowheads, spearheads and many human skeletons were found.

After examining these houses, follow the path to the hill top. Now you are standing on the paved terrace of the Temple of Athena. Look across the impressive plain of Troy where the war took place and the Dardanelles and Gallipoli Peninsula on the other side of the straits where one of the bloodiest battles of the First World War took place.

When you are looking at the Dardanelles, if you can imagine the Allied fleet which tried to sail through the Straits during the First World War, you may remember the famous British battleship "AGAMEMNON". This name may remind you of the resemblence of the two wars. At the east end of this terrace you can see the northern tower of Troy VI and the well-cistern in it. The square well next to it belonged to the Temple of Athena. As you are looking towards the tower, raising your head you see trees and bushes. Despite the trees you can recognize the site of the main theatre shaped like a big bow. On the other side of this bow are the wooden excavation houses used by the archaeologists, called "Bademli köy" (Almond village).

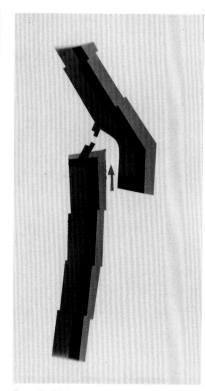

Detailed Plan of The East Gate

Turning back again to the terrace, before you walk down to the big trench dug by Schliemann, see the stones on the other side of the trench and imagine that the trench in front of you was covered with stone slabs like those you are standing on, before Schliemann excavated it. Walk down into the large pit. After a few steps you come to a heavy piece of marble ceiling sculptured with flowers. You can see some other pieces and huge marble columns here and there. Observing them, you can picture the size of the Doric temple of Athena. But unfortunately that is all that is left of the most important building of this city. We do not know at what time the temple was built, but we know that it was built on the orders of Alexander the Great as he was passing by Troy in 334 BC. This Hellenistic temple was partly destroyed in 85 BC during Fimbria's sack of Troy, later re-erected with the financial support of Augustus. Julius Caesar worshipped in it and paid great attention to enlarging it and making it more magnificent.

Following the path through the marble columns and capitals, just after the first unexcavated island of earth with a stone wall, you are in front of the main gate of Troy I. Here you see the fortification wall of Troy I made of small unworked stones with a sloping outer face. The top part of this 5000 year old wall was made of sun-dried bricks. Remember that in this Early Bronze Age period, iron tools were not used. Leaving this gate behind, continue along the path by the unexcavated cone which has been covered by stones and mud to protect it against erosion for future generations. As you walk note some foundations on your right side. The foundations belong to the biggest megaron of Troy II. The walls of these megaron houses, which had square plans, were built of

Small Houses of Troy VIIa

mud bricks over stone foundations and every house had an entrance hall. The mud brick wall of this biggest megaron was excavated in 1991. The 4500 year old plastered wall was found in good condition and to preserve it for the future it was buried again.

Continue along the path to the west, on your right you can see the house walls of Troy I. Note the stone work of these parallel walls. You can easily observe the herring bone pattern on one of the foundations. The new mud brick wall and the sloping wall above it were built by the new excavation team to protect the foundations from falling stones. The new excavations are being carried on, at the northern end of this trench. Evidence of a new settlement under Troy 1 was found in this trench.

Passing over the wooden bridge behind you, observe the different phases of Troy II city walls and plastered reconstruction of a tower of early Troy II. Opposite the bridge you can see the new excavated trench with different layers. The path after the bridge will take you to a ramp. Advance up to the steps and turn back to examine the ramp. This ramp paved with large stones and the walls on both sides of it are 4500 years old. The walls are massive but made of rough stones. Here imagine that this ramp ran directly beneath a huge tower through a large covered corridor. Foundations of this covered corridor and tower were reconstructed at the end of the 1992 excavation season.

Needless to say, the trench at the north west end of this ramp is one of Schliemann's trenches. Note how he cut down through the later lavels. Schliemann discovered the famous treasure, which he called "the treasure of Priam", in this trench, just by the city wall of Troy II. He unearthed it alone without his workmen, and with his wife's help he carried the treasure away. He smuggled it first to Greece and then to Berlin. Since the Second World War no one knew the where abouts of the treasure until 1993 when it was re-discovered in Pushkin Museum in Moscow. Let us listen to him with his own words:

"While following up to the circuit wall, and bringing more and more of it to light, I struck at a point slightly northwest of the gate, a large copper article of the most remarkable form, which attracted my attention all the more as I thought I saw gold glimmering behind it. On the top was a layer of reddish and brown calcined ruins from 4 to 5 feet thick as hard as stone, and above this again the wall of fortification, which must have been erected shortly after the destruction of Troy. In order to secure the treasure from my workmen and save it for archaeology, it was necessary to lose no time; so although it was not yet the hour for breakfast, I immediately had the "paidos" (interval for rest) called, and while the men were eating and resting I cut out the treasure with a large knife. This involved risk, as the fortification wall beneath which I had to dig, threatened every moment to fall on my head. And indeed I should not

A House Troy VI

The Platform Of The Temple of Athena

North-Eastern Tower of Troy VI

have succeeded in getting posses-
sion of the treasure without the
help of my wife, who stood at
my side, ready to pack the
things I cut in her shawl, and to
carry them away. As I found all
these articles together packed
into one another in the form of
a rectangular mass, it seems
certain that they were placed inside a wooden chest"

Ilios PP. 40, 41

Climbing up to the steps you
reach Troy VI level again. Here
there is only one way to go. On
your right side lies the western
unit of the fortification wall of
Troy VI. Observing this wall with
the help of your map try to find
the location of the western
gate. The gate is closed today
with unworked stones. If you
compare the rough stones with
the handsome walls on both
sides, you can see the difference, imagine that in place of
those rough stones, there was
a gate which was called the
West Gate. Possibly this was
the famous gate through which
the wooden horse was pulled
into the citadel. If you observe
the walls carefully, you will see
traces of widening the gate to
take the huge wooden horse
into the citadel. After the Trojans took the horse in, instead
of repairing the gateway which
would take time, they closed it
quickly by using rough stones.
This interpretation may make
sense for those who believe the
wooden horse story took place,
as told in the legend. Though it
has not been proved by the archaeologists we find it interesting.
Walk a little bit further from the
west gate. You come to an interesting house which looks like
a small fortress with its segmented, sloping and finely constructed walls. Looking at these
walls you can easily understand
that this is a house from Troy
VI. This house was called the
"Palace of Priam" by Schliemann. But it was possibly used
as a storage house in Troy VIIa

Ceiling Block of The Temple Of Athena

Unexcavated Cone

Fortification Wall of Troy I

House Walls of Troy I

because many big storage jars of Troy VIIa were found in it.

Follow the path to the right of this house, to see the holy place of the Hellenistic age, which is surrounded by a typical Hellenic Wall. The lower rounded foundations indicate that here there was an earlier sanctuary before the Greek period. The marble construction which has a square plan is an altar from Hellenistic and Roman times. Another altar with a sacrifical pit is from the early Greek period. Here you see two wells. The well closer to the sacrificial area is a blood well. It has a hole at ground level to take the blood into the well. the other well is a water well.

According to Herodotus, Persian King Xerxes sacrificed 1000 oxen here to Athena, a Greek goddess, on his way to Greece. (480 B.C.). This great offering to an enemy god was a sort of bribe. Leaving behind the sanctuary follow the path to the left. You come to a Roman Bath on the right. The floor of this bath was once completely covered with beautiful mosaics depicting figures of men and animals and a figure of a bowl of fruit made of coloured stones. But unfortunately nothing is left of this mosaic.

Opposite the bath you see a small theatre. This is a Roman odeon, a music theatre. It was built on the sloping outer face of the fortification wall of Troy VI. Note the changing room to the left of the stage and the marble seats for the lord of the city. This was probably built at the end of the first century A.D. Decorated marble blocks in front of the odeon were part of the stage.

Behind the odeon, you can observe some house walls of Troy VIIa by the city walls, also a large house of which one of the stone pillars is still in its original place, to support the second storey.

Advancing a little further from the odeon, you come to the south gate and south tower of Troy VI and VIIa. The south gate was the principal gate for both

The New Excavations At Schliemann's North-South Trench

Paved Ramp of Troy II

So Called "Palace Of Priam"

Troy VI and VIIa. Probably this gate is the "Scaean gate" where the Achilles-Hector duel took place. Note the drainage gutter in the middle of the street which was used to take the rain water out of the acropolis. Some square bases probably for statues of gods are still in their original places just by the tower.

The fortification wall on the right side of the south gate was badly damaged by construction of a Roman bouleuterion (senate). Today only the stage and the first row of marble seating of this Augustian building can be seen. The other seats made of sandstone are not in good condition. The stones unearthed at the end of the 1991 excavation season were numbered and collected in front of this building. Passing by these stones you return to the spot where you started.

Now it is time to enjoy climbing the wooden horse and taking pictures.

Holy Place Troy VIII

Roman Bath

A Reconstruction of The South Gate

Drainage Gutter

HEINRICH SCHLIEMANN

Heinrich Schliemann, a German businessman who was born in 1822 in Mecklenburg, read the Iliad by heart at a very young age. He was blessed with enough imagination to discover Troy, and felt the excitement of the Trojan War deeply. While many people thought that Troy was only a legendary city which never existed, Schliemann believed every line of the Iliad. He accepted the Trojan War as an historical fact, and learned several languages in order to understand the Iliad better. To make the world believe the existence of Troy, with the guidence of Homer he started making plans to discover Troy.

First of all he needed limitless money for it was necessary to see the world and support the excavations. Thanks to his enthusiasm, as well as his great luck, he made four immense fortunes at various times in his life. Especially by supplying materials for the Russian army through the blackmarket, during the Crimean war, and by banking in California during the gold-rush.

After solving the money problem, now he was ready for archaeology. Besides exploring Troy, one of his childhood dreams was to see the Great Wall of China. So he went there first. By hiring private guides he visited the great wall. He enjoyed climbing it and measured the bricks. Detaching a brick from the wall and carrying it all the way down with great effort was his first serious encounter with archaeology(!) The guides laughed at him, because of the trouble he had carrying a solitary brick, but we do not think they would tolerate this in today's understanding of archaeology.

The China visit took Schliemann away from thoughts of Troy. He visited almost half the countries in the world, and learned 12 or 13 languages. He had three children by his Russian wife. By now he was a 43 year old weary man with grey hair. But still he had no idea what he would do with his life. Should he become a writer or a philologist? He was restless and unhappy. He went to America again, but he could not stay there long and went back to Paris. In Paris he attended important meetings with his mistress and led a luxurious life. But nothing appeased him. Why was he living? Why was he unhappy? Why was he always wandering around the world like a homeless beggar?

While he was asking himself these questions, the memories of Homer which had enchanted his childhood filled him again. Did not Odysseus wander so many years and return to Ithaca and meet his wife Penelope? Did not he enter his own home disguised as a beggar on his return from his long wanderings?

He suddenly decided to go to Greece. He thought he might find his own Penelope there. That would stop his wanderings. From the moment he set foot on Ithaca he was like a man enchanted. He had to go everywhere and see everything. Inspite of the heat he was deliriously happy. In a short time he organised a small team consisting of a donkey and four workers, and started to dig at Mount Aetios. He found 20 vases containing ashes. He was sure they were human ashes. One of these urns might well contain the ashes of Odysseus and Penelope or their descendants. This easy success led him to believe in his innate ability as an archaeologist and whetted his appetite for archaeology. He worked by instinct and enthusiasm. After further fruitless excavations he went to Mycenae, Tiryns and Athens and later set out for Troy by way of Istanbul.

The Russian consul obtained a guide and two horses for him. As he wandered over the plain of Troy he was in high spirits, pleased to see the storks flapping their wings on the roofs of the houses.

He went to Pınarbaşı, which was long believed to be the site of Troy. After doing research there he decided that Pınarbaşı was not the place.

Frank Calvert, an Englishman who acted as American vice-consul for the Dardanelles, had done some preliminary digging at Hisarlık. Believing that he had found Troy, he invited the British Museum to begin excavations. He wanted the British to have the honour of discovering Troy, but nothing came of his proposals. When Schliemann came he decided to help him as much as he could. He took him through the site and showed him the remains of a temple formed of great blocks of hewn stone which he had excavated by himself.

Schliemann concentrated on Hi-sarlık. Everything fitted in well with the Iliad. All that was needed was to remove these great stone blocks and find the ruins of Priam's marble palace and his treasure. He discussed his theories and plans for the excavations with Calvert. He was in a mood for quick action. But it was already late in the season for digging. Permission also had to be obtained from the Turkish Government.

Calvert was amused by Schliemann's wild enthusiasm. He owned half of the Hisarlık hill and generously promised to help him. His generosity, so unlike a merchant, confused Schliemann. He knew that without Calvert he would not be able to do anything. On his return home he wrote many letters to Calvert demanding answers to many questions such as what sort of a hat he should wear. How many workers should he employ? Should he choose them from the Turks or the Greeks? The cost of the excavations and so on.

As he was preparing himself for the excavations, he was looking for a suitable wife who would accompany him during the excavations. He had divorced his Russian wife and decided upon a Greek bride because he liked the sound of the language, especially when spoken by women. In his diary one day he wrote as follows:

"I am intoxicated by this language, it surprises me that a language can be so noble! I do not know what others think but it seems to me there must be a great future for Greece, and the day can not be far distant when the Hellenic flag will fly over Sancta Sophia!"

In addition to this absurd prophecy, he also wrote:

"What amazes me more than anything else is that the Greeks, after three centuries of Turkish domination, still preserve their national language intact".

As he was writing this he never considered that this was because of the boundless tolerance by the Turks for other nations and cultures. He was travelling everywhere with Greek books and saw the world through Greek eyes, and became a fanatical champion of Greek claims to Constantinopole, the "megalo idea". So a Greek wife would be ideal for him. But how to find one? He decided to write a letter to Vimpos, a Greek priest. Describing her qualifications, he wrote:

"She should be poor, beautiful, a Homer enthusiast dark haired, well educated and possessed of a good and loving heart". Vimpos collected photographs of suitable young Athenian girls and sent them to Schliemann. He chose the picture of a 17 year old girl named Sophia and decided to meet her. He visited Sophia's familiy and questioned her carefully. She was beautiful but how about the other things? He enquired,

"Would you like to go on long journeys?" The answer was yes. After getting the right answer to a history question, she had to recite passages from Homer by

A Golden Mask Found in Mycenae

Sophia Schliemann Wearing A Diadem Found at Troy

Similar Diadem of The Present Troad

heart. Sophia did and passed the examination. In a short time he married Sophia and turned to the subject of Troy.

He wrote letters to Calvert. Although he could not get permission for excavations, he left Sophia in Athens and came to Troy.

The eastern part of the mound belonged to Frank Calvert, the western part belonged to two Turks living at Kumkale. Believing that the most important buildings were in the western part overlooking the sea, he started to dig from the west with ten workers. He was so sure of finding great buildings and treasure that he did not even get permission from the Turks. He thought they would forgive his audacity when they saw the treasure and large buildings.

The first day he uncovered foundations of a house. The second day, with eleven more workmen, he uncovered the whole house. Among the cinders he found a coin bearing on one side the image of Hector with the inscription 'Hector of Troy'. In Schliemann's eyes this was the most auspicious sign of all. On the third day, fearing that the Turkish landowners might arrive at any moment, he made two long trenches, one from east to west and another from south to north. By slicing across the top of the mound he hoped to form a general picture of the buried city.

Schliemann was right. The Turks arrived soon. They asked him what he was doing on their property. Schliemann explained through an interpreter that he was doing scientific work and the results of this would be profitable for Turkey. He was pleading and giving long explanations about his discoveries but the Turks were more interested in the heavy blocks of stone he had unearthed. They intended building a stone bridge over one of the rivers nearby and these blocks suited their purpose exactly. Schliemann would let them take the stones for the bridge.

He also paid them forty francs. They agreed to let Schliemann continue digging. But he knew that this truce was temporary. After getting enough stones for their bridge, they ordered him to stop digging. They also demanded 100 pounds for the damage he had caused. Of course he refused to pay but he had no defence against their ultimatum. As he was leaving Hisarlık he understood that he had to buy the hill. For this he wrote letters to some important people in Germany, France, Athens and Istanbul. In a letter to Safvet Pasha, the Turkish minister of Culture, he tried to explain that he was not a "treasure hunter." His only desire was to prove that the city of Troy was beneath the mound at Hisarlık. He desired permission only for that. Meanwhile Frank Calvert had obtained from the two Turkish landowners a verbal promise that they would sell their property to Schliemann for 1000 francs. But Safvet Pasha bought the land for 600 francs on behalf of the ministry.

This was not the solution he wanted. He was extremely angry. He wrote letters to Calvert, to find a way to buy the land. He offered to give all the gold and silver treasure he discovered to the ministry. He would even give Safvet Pasha double the value of the precious metals he might find. But he insisted he would not dig unless he was given title to the land. Nothing worked. This time he came up with a new offer. He made no claim on the land, he only wanted permission to find the city of Priam. He did not want any money but he would be very happy to divide the precious objects, one half for the museum, the other half for his own collection, to cover his expenses. As he was asking permission to take his share out of the country, with his Odysseuslike cunning, he said he did not expect to find any treasure there.

This last letter, written with the help of American Ambassador, solved all the problems. Poison was mingled with honey within it. On 12 August 1871 when he was in London the "ferman" containing the permission reached him and soon he started excavating at Hisarlık. For the first time he attacked Hisarlık with the full protection of the Turkish government. The rains came, and they were still working. The number of workers was increasing day by day. The number of workmen reached 120. He was in a hurry to find the pallace of Priam. But the things he found were not satisfactory. They all belonged to later periods. He could not find anything from the time of Priam. One day he found a relief of Apollo riding the four horses of the sun. Though small, it was a brilliant piece of work. He smuggled it out of the country with the help of Frank Calvert. For years it graced the garden of Schliemann's house in Athens.

Schliemann reached his goal in May 1873. As he was standing near to a trench with Sophia, he suddenly noticed some metal objects. He was sure that he had found treasure. The question was how to protect it from the workmen. None of the workmen had noticed it. Sophia was beside him, and he turned to her and said:

"You must go at once and shout PAIDOS". Paidos was a Greek word, as well as Turkish, meaning "rest period".

Sophia had not yet seen the treasure, and was amazed at the thought of ordering a rest period so early.

"Now, at seven o'clock?" She asked.

"Yes - now!" said Schliemann. "Tell them it is my birthday, and I have only just remembered it! Tell them they will get their wages today without working. See that they go to their villages and see that the overseer does not come here. Hurry, and shout "paidos". "Sophia did as she was told. The workmen were pleased with this unexpected holiday. Amin Efendi, the Turkish representative, was a little puzzled, because he was usually well informed about holidays, but he too obeyed "paidos".

Apollo Riding The Four Horses of The Sun

The Big Treasure

After all the workmen had gone, Sophia returned to the trench where Schliemann was attempting to dig the treasure out with a pocket knife, in danger from collapsing stones and earth. After a while he turned again to Sophia and said:

"Quick, bring me your big shawl!"

Sophia returned with a big shawl. The treasure was put into the shawl and together they carried it back to the wooden house.

The treasure consisted of a copper shield, a copper cauldron, a silver vase and another of copper, a gold bottle, two gold cups, and a small electrum cup. There was a silver goblet, three great silver vases, seven double-edged copper daggers, six silver knife blades, and thirteen copper lance-heads, two gold diadems, fifty-six gold earrings, 8750 gold rings and buttons. The two diadems, one of them consisting of ninety chains, entirely covering the forehead, were exceptional. Nothing like them had ever been seen before.

Amin Efendi was suspicious. Rumours were flying around the Trojan plain. He called at Schliemann's house and angrily proclaimed he was sure something was being kept from him. Amin Efendi demanded permission to search the house. In the name of the sultan he ordered Schliemann to open all his chests, even the wardrobes. Schliemann threw him out of the house.

That night or the next night, six baskets and one bag, containing the treasure and other objects found previously, were taken to Calvert's farm house near Pınarbaşı. Calvert's farm, called Kumkale farm, is a state farm today.

In a few days the treasure and other things were smuggled out of the country with the help of Calvert.

Staying a few more days at Hisarlık, Schliemann peered and probed the trench, believed that no more treasure was left, terminated the excavations abruptly and returned to Athens. What he left behind was a desolate mound riddled with corridors and trenches like a battlefield. From Athens he started writing letters to all learned societies in Europe saying that he had made "the greatest discovery of our age". With great enthusiasm and excitement he declared that the treasure he had found was the "treasure of Priam" and Hisarlık hill was the legendary "city of Priam". Using the treasure as a lever he started bargaining with the Greek government. He said he would give it to Greece if they give him full permission to excavate at Mycenae and Olympia. The Greeks refused because they were afraid of trouble with Turkey.

Meanwhile Amin Efendi was put in prison because he had failed to keep close watch on the excavations. On the other hand the Turks asked Schliemann privately to send the fair share of the objects to the Imperial Museum in Istanbul, according to the agreement. Schliemann an-

swered that he would send nothing. Then the Turks instituted proceedings against him for half of the treasure. The trial lasted a year in Athens. The Greek judges found in favour of the Turks and ordered him to pay 50.000 francs. Schliemann thought the value of the treasure was about one million Francs. Now it was time for Schliemann to act with the cunning of Odysseus and play his cards skilfuly. As a gesture of friendship he sent five times the amount of the indemnity to the Archaeological Museum in Istanbul. He also sent seven large vases and four sacks filled with stone implements which were found in Troy. That was enough to melt the ice between the Turks and Schliemann. The skilled merchant had won his victory. He demanded new permission from Safvet Pasha and got it in April 1876. Meanwhile the Greek government also gave him permission to excavate. Thinking that it was early for Troy, he returned to Greece and started excavating at Mycenae.

In Mycenae he was lucky again. He found some golden masks in a grave near the Lions Gate. He called one of them "the Mask of Agamemnon". Later he excavated Odysseus' palace in Ithaca but could not find anything valuable and abandoned the excavations.

Troy summoned him again. It was his sixth journey to Troy. This time he was not alone. Many scholars believed that he had discovered Troy. Some famous archaeologists joined the excavations and more serious work was done. The Turkish government sent a special commissioner and ten policemen to Hisarlık to superintend the excavations. On October 21, 1878 he found treasure, consisting of 20 gold earrings, a number of gold spiral rings, 2 heavy bracelets of electrum, 11 silver earrings, 158 silver rings and a large number of gold beads. A few days later he found another smaller hoard. This time he was allowed to keep only a

third of the treasure he found; the rest went to the Archeological museum in Istanbul.

The following year he found a few earrings and bracelets. That was all. He found no more treasure. His luck was not holding. He was also growing old. He returned to Athens and built a house, designed by himself, in the middle of Athens. He called it 'The palace of Troy'.

Later many scientists visited Troy. Many scientific congresses were held there in the presence of Schliemann. On an excursion to Mount Ida he was soaked to the skin in a rainstorm. After that the terrible pain in his ears which had started previously became worse. Even after an operation the pain returned, more terrible than ever. It would cause his death. Against the advice of the doctors he decided to leave the hospital.

Schliemann died in Naples in 1890. His coffin was transported to Athens and he was buried there on a place opposite the Acropolis according to his will.

After Schliemann's death, his best friend, the young architect Wilhelm Dörpfeld, went on excavating at Hisarlık. Dörpfeld always insisted that everything had to be photographed, labelled and minutely examined before it was thrown away. Being always in hurry, Schliemann refused to do this as he thought it was a waste of time.

The real systematic excavations at Troy started with Wilhelm Dörpfeld. The first plan of Troy was done by him. But the most detailed work was done by Karl Blegen from the Cincinnati expedition. The Americans started excavating in 1932 and spent about seven seasons at Troy. Examining even the smallest details, they continued this careful work until 1939.

Blegen separated the different levels and examined the remains of the nine cities. He also dated them according to the fire traces, ceramics and buildings but mostly according to historical events.

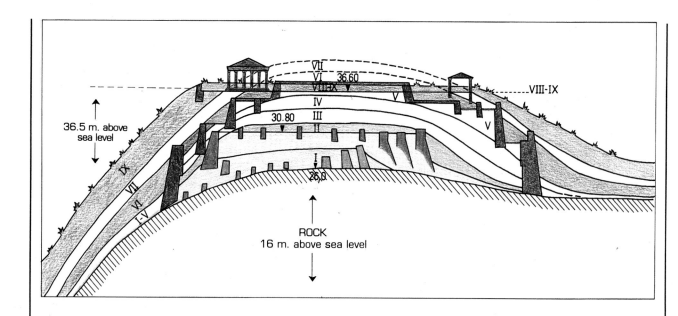

CULTURAL STRATA

TROY I. (3000 - 2500 B.C.)

The first inhabitants of Troy built their houses on a 16 m. high, indigeneous rock at the western end of the ridge. The city was fortified by a wall made of rough stones. Today we can see only a short segment of this wall, some 12 m. long, and the main gate with two square towers. The thickness of the fortification wall is about 2.50 m. The other remains of the first Troy we can see today are some foundations of houses in Schliemann's north-south trench. These houses were long believed to be megaron houses. But according to the latest research they do not have megaron plans. Manfred Korfmann, the head of the latest excavation team, who cleared the trench and made some re-constructions there in 1988, calls them "row of long houses". "Megarons", the prototype of the Greek temples, were free-standing houses consisting of a single room with an entrance hall. But these long and narrow houses, which were built of mudbricks over stone founda-tions, were not free standing houses. Some of them had the entrance in the corner. The stone foundation walls of some

The Tower And The City Wall of Troy I

of these houses were built in herringbone style. Although this type of workmanship is seen in Mesopotamia too, there was no direct influence since it was already known all over Anatolia and can be seen even today on the walls of some Turkish houses. We can also see the same design very often in the ceramics of Troy I.

We do not know much about the building technique but we think the fish bone designs on their ceramics show us that the artisans might well be influenced by their daily life. Fishing was a very important occupation for the first inhabitants of Troy. A fishing hook made of copper, which was found recently in the ruins of Troy I, strengthens this opinion.

In one of these long houses two infant burials were found just beneath the floor. One of them was in a shallow pit covered by a flat stone, the other one was in an urn. More examples of the same type of burial have been uncovered in open spaces in the city, but no adult burials were encountered in the acropolis. This can be explained by children's need for protection. They believed that babies, especially new-born babies, needed protection even after death. This is why babies were buried in the houses or in the gardens, and adults outside the city walls.

The Early Bronze Age inhabitants of Troy I made their tools of copper, stone and bone. Stone vessels and pottery were in constant use. All pots were shaped by hand, without the use of the potter's wheel.

Some spindle whorls and loom weights have been found, showing that spinning and weaving were familiar occupations for these natives of north western Asia Minor.

Troy I, which had ten building phases, was eventually wiped out by a great fire.

TROY II. (2500 - 2300 B.C.)

The second settlement at Hisarlık was built on top of the ruins of Troy I. It seems that the inhabitants of Troy I. completely reconstructed the citadel after the disaster. There is evidence that the culture of Troy I. continued in this period. Megarons were the general style of houses. Some of them were quite large and some of them had more rooms but the design was basically the same.

During recent excavations, a wall from the biggest megaron was uncovered, under a cone which was used as a measuring point and left unexcavated by Schliemann. The cone was excavated by Prof. Günter Mansfeld, one of the archeologists in the German team. As well as some findings belonging to different periods, the mudbrick wall of the biggest megaron - which can be accepted as the palace of Troy II - was unearthed. The plaster of the brick wall was

The Long Row of Houses of Troy I

found in very good condition. Due to a great fire the plaster and the bricks turned red. This 4500 year old palace wall was buried again at the end of the 1991 excavation season to preserve it for future generations.

Troy II had a roughly circular plan about 110 m. in diameter. It was a little larger than Troy I. The powerful defensive fortification wall was built of relatively small unworked stones and had a broadly sloping outer face. Sloping walls are stronger against earthquakes and easier to built. The upper part of the wall was supported by a vertical superstructure of sundried brick. Small rectangular towers, at intervals of approximately 10 m. would have strengthened the defensive arrangements. In some places the wall is seen to have been built in separate parallel sections. These are the different building phases of Troy II. One of the early Troy II. towers was reconstructed in 1992.

There were two main gates; one on the southeast, the other one on the southwest. Both display a peculiar plan with fairly large covered corridors which ran directly beneath a huge tower and jutted out from the wall. The sides of the corridor were shored up with vertical timbers. They presumably also supported transverse beams to prevent the stonework of the tower falling into the corridor.

The southwestern gateway is better preserved and the roadway, which was paved with great slabs of limestone, rose 5m. to the level of the gate by means of a ramp 21 m. long and 7.55m wide which was bordered on each side by a stone wall. It was however too steep for wheeled traffic. The southeastern gate has the same plan as the southwestern except for the paved ramp. There is another small gateway about 8m. long and 5m. wide to the south which leads to a cobbled court. The

findings show us that the inhabitants of Troy II. had quite a high standard of living. The treasure found by Schliemann of gold, silver, electron (an alloy of gold and silver) and bronze all belong to this period. Objects included among this treasure make it clear that the women of this time led a life of relative luxury. The artisans who made these handicrafts were very skilful. The potters started using the potter's wheel and made beautiful ceramics. Two-handled depas for wine were characteristic pots of this period.

A vast amount of jewelary and traces of fire led Schliemann to believe that this level was the Troy of Priam and Homer. Later, with the help of architect Wilhelm Dörpfeld, he accepted Troy VI as the city of Priam. However the American expedition concluded that the Troy of Priam was level VIIa.

Troy II was burned down by a warrior nation.

Reconstruction of Troy II

Paved Ramp

TROY III. IV. V. (2300 - 1700 B.C.)

After the disaster that brought Troy II. to an end, the survivors rebuilt the whole town. The absence of any fresh influence from outside the Troad indicates that there was no break in cultural continuity. The same people followed the same way of life and clung to the same traditions.

Probably the invaders of Troy II. left this place and emigrated somewhere else, or mixing with the natives they lost their own character and lived together, for a long era, through Troy III. Troy IV. and Troy V. till the end of the Early Bronze Age.

Although each of these settlements had a greater population and occupied a larger area, none could create a better civilisation than its predecessor. Each was like a village with irregular blocks of houses, seperated by narrow streets. This can be explained in terms of people living in fear of another disaster. Actually during this period Anatolia had many invasions. The Hittites in particular became a great power at this time. Because Schliemann removed all the walls of these periods, there are hardly any re-

Early Troy II Tower

mains left today, nor do we know what brought each of them to an end.

During recent excavations in the southern part of Schliemann's north-south trench some sturdy walls were uncovered. These walls, which look like defence walls, may be the city walls of these periods. Further excavations will enable us to get more information about these periods.

Depas for Wine

Stone Axes

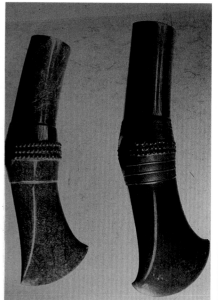

TROY VI (1700-1250 B.C.)

The findings of Troy VI. indicate to us a break with the past and a course of gradual change and development. Powerful fortifications and free standing houses show that these people were highly advanced in military engineering, masonry and town planning.

Today we can only see the remains of the fortification wall and a few houses, along the outer periphery of the acropolis. In the central part of the citadel there are almost no remains of Troy VI, because the top of the mound was shaved off in Hellenistic and Roman times in order to provide an open court around the temple of Athena.

The monumental fortification walls of Troy VI, and its towers, were built of squared blocks of hard durable limestone. There are five gateways, which were designated Vlu, Vlv, Vlt, Vls, and Vlr.

The main eastern gateway is a passage about 2m. wide and 5m. long between overlapping walls. At the end of this corridor the gateway turns sharply inward and here there was once actually a door that could be opened and closed. As seen today, it was very well planned to resist attack.

The southwestern part of the wall and its tower, which we see at the entrance of the ruins today, is still in good condition. But the southern part of this wall was badly damaged when a roman bouleuterion (senate) was built over it. On this wall, large limestone blocks were freely used in the lower part; smaller stones in the upper. The sloping outer face of the wall was divided into straight segments by vertical offsets.

What were these vertical offsets for? Were they merely decorative or had they some purpose?

An American architect I guided through the ruins gave me one possible explanation which seems to make sense. He suggested that the Trojans constructed the city wall, block by block and that the offsets were intended to disguise the weakest part of the construction, the point where two blocks interlocked. The offsets are carved so as to be easy for an enemy to observe, the intention was presumably to give an attacker a false impression of the strength of the weakest part of the wall. But the existence of the same sort of carving on a house wall inside the city walls, make us believe that in fact it was merely decorative. Some visitors I guide through the site believe that this was an extraordinary effort just for decoration.

It is true that this was no easy

Reconstruction of Troy VI

Sloping Walls of Troy VI

House with Columns Troy VI

task for the bronze age, when they did not have iron tools, but throughout history men have gone to great time and expense merely for decoration.

The tower was added to this wall later as further protection for the east gate. If you compare the masonary of the wall and the tower you can easily see the different workmanship.

The northeastern tower is a huge tower with very handsome stonework. Inside is a well or cistern. It is too large to be an ordinary well, too deep for an ordinary cistern. Probably it was built for both purposes. This tower was built as an observation tower, dominating not only the acropolis but the whole Trojan plain, as well as enclosing the well-cistern within the fortification, thus ensuring a safe supply of water in emergencies. On the south part of the tower there is a side gate that facilitated communication between the tower and the outside world. The stairway on the northern side of the tower is in good condition but it is believed that this was built in the Hellenistic period.

The wall between the northeastern tower and the east gate was cut across by a Roman foundation.

The southern gate is the prin-

The Eastern Gate Of Troy VI from Inside

cipal entrance to the fortress. It was a simple opening, 3.30 m. wide with a relatively broad street which ascended from the gate towards the citadel. The gateway was protected by a tower about 7 m. wide. It is exactly the same as the eastern tower. We wonder if this was the famous gate mentioned in the Iliad as the "Scaean gate" where the duel between Achilles and Hector took place. Between the south gate and southwest gate, for a distance of some 121 m., lies the southern part of the fortification wall. The greater part of this wall was badly damaged by the construction of a small odeon and other public buildings in the late classical and Roman times. At the west end of this wall there was a gateway which for some reason was later blocked up. What could this reason be?

Today we all accept that the fortification walls of Troy VI were used during Troy VIIa. The American expedition proved that the Troy of Priam was the first Phase of Troy VII. According to Prof. Fritz Schachermeyr, the Austrian archeologist, and Prof. Ekrem Akurgal, the Turkish archeologist, Troy VI was the city of Priam. Whether it was VI. or VII. the same city walls were used in both periods. That means these walls are certainly the walls of Priam's city.

In the light of this knowledge and with the help of a little imagination, the blocking up can be explained by the wooden horse story. As we take this mythological approach, we want to make you think, though as yet this theory cannot be proved. In fact, if we examine this gate carefully, we can see evidence of its having been enlarged. That is, the Trojans tore down the wall to enlarge the gate to take the huge wooden horse into the citadel. Soon after this, instead of re-building the gate, which would have taken time, they completely closed it off using unworked stones.

This explanation makes sense if the wooden horse story actually occured as told in the legend, otherwise there must be another explanation.

Free standing houses of different designs and megaron-like large houses were characteristic of this period. The pillared house, a megaron with the roof supported by wooden pillars, was introduced. Examining these houses and others, we can say that building techniques reached their full development and some powerful authority controlled the planning of the houses in the acropolis.

At this level black and grey Minoan pottery has been found in a wide variety of characteristic shapes.

Troy VI was brought to its end by a violent earthquake.

Northern Tower Of Troy VI

Principal Entrance of Troy VI

TROY VIIa (1250-1180 B.C.)

After the earthquake that laid Troy VI in ruins, the survivors immediately repaired the fortification walls, reconstructed the old houses and built many new ones. The same people continued to occupy the same place through Troy VIIa with a direct, unbroken continuation of the culture of Troy VI.

After the earthquake, the upper part of the great wall was rebuilt and some additions were made. On the eastern side of the fortress a new wall was added to the older wall which overlapped the east gateway, but this extension was destroyed during the excavations.

The south gateway was also repaired and it continued to be the principal entrance to the citadel. The way through the opening was paved with large flat stones. In the middle of the paved area an underground drain was made at this time. This drain, which was made to carry off rain water from the upper part of the acropolis, can still be seen today.

The houses which were found within the outer ring of the acropolis were smaller and roughly built, because the acropolis at this time was obliged to shelter a larger population than its predecessor. The walls were thick and sturdy, but no real effort was made to build handsome structures.

In this period in almost every house, large storage jars were set deeply into the ground and covered with a heavy stone slab. The size of these jars ranged from 1.75m. to 2m. in height and 1m. to 1.25m. in diameter. These large jars were regularly used for the storage of solids - as well as liquid supplies for an emergency.

The numerous small, roughly built houses everywhere in the acropolis and innumerable storage jars indicate that a large number of people sheltered within the fortification from an invasion. This and some traces of fire and fighting like arrow heads and spear heads on the walls and abundance of human skeletons. Especially a human jaw cut by a sword - makes us think that Troy VIIa was the Troy of Priam which was besieged and captured by the Achaens and destroyed by fire.

This is the opinion of the American Cincinnatti University team but according to Prof. F. Schachermeyr and Prof. Ekrem Akurgal, Troy VI was the city of Priam. With fine fortifications, ingenious design and carefully constructed buildings, Troy VI

fits in well with the Iliad.

"Priam and his sons Paris and Hector or else the king and princes known to us by their names in myth, must have lived during this glorious period. To take this powerful city the Greeks fought for ten years. They could only achieve their goal after the city had been destroyed by an earthquake. Since the Greeks well knew that they owed their victory to Poseidon, the Earthshaker, they offered him a wooden horse for his great help"
(E. Akurgal, Ancient civilizations and Ruins of Turkey 1973)
The horse was the symbol of Poseidon.

TROY VIIb. (1180-1000 B.C.)
After the departure of the Achaens, the citadel was reoccupied by the survivors. The first phase of Troy VIIb followed the same way of life as Troy VIIa. but later changed as a result of migrations. This stratum too was destroyed by fire.

A Strorage Jar

TROY VIII. (1000-85 B.C.)

Troy VIII was the first Greek settlement in Troy. At this time Greek culture was dominant and this stratum was a typical Greek colony. A religious area with a place for worshipping and sacrificing, just outside the western part of the Troy VI city wall, was built in this period. The Persian king Xerxes stayed here and sacrificed 1000 oxen to the Greek gods on his way to Greece (480 B.C.)

After bribing the enemy gods with the 1000 oxen, Xerxes had a bridge of ships built over the Dardanelles. But the bridge was destroyed by the strong current. Then he punished the Dardanelles by whipping the waters 300 times (!) Later two new bridges were built. One for the animals, the other for the soldiers.

Alexander the Great, on his way to Granicus, stayed here and made valuable offerings. (334 B.C.) He also ordered Lysimachus, one of his commanders, to build the Temple of Athena.

The New Addition to The Older Wall Troy VIIa

Sanctuary Troy VIII

TROY IX (85 B.C. - 400 or 600 A.D.)

The top stratum, which was built on the ruins of the earlier settlements at Hisarlık, was a Hellenistic and Roman city. This last settlement which is known as "Novum Ilium" or New "Ilion" made great progress at the time of the early Roman emperors. The great Roman emperors chose the Trojans as their ancestors. Augustus especially showed great interest in the city and enlarged and beautified the Temple of Athena.

Also at this time the town spread all over the ridge and was bigger than it had ever been in its long history.

To supply water for the city, water pipes and aqueducts were built. An aqueduct which is still in good condition can be seen today in Kemerdere village, 14 km. from Troy, on the mountainside.

The greater part of the city is still unexcavated. In the excavated area, a roman odeon (music theatre) and a bouleuterion (council chamber-senate), built over the southern part of the fortification wall of Troy VI, can be seen. Also a Roman bath opposite the odeon and a few marble pieces of the Temple of Athena.

Only eight rows of seats from the odeon are relatively well preserved. The marble seat on the eighth row was the imperial box and the changing room on the left of the stage was marble surfaced same as the orchestra.

The odeon was probably a covered construction, for there is no channel for rain water.

The floor of the Roman bath was once covered with beautiful mosaics. The bath and the mo-

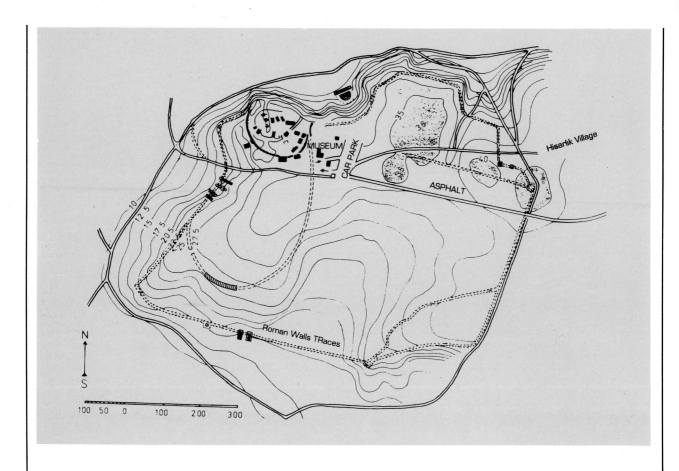

saics were uncovered by the Cincinnati team. The mosaics were not protected and tourists took them as small souvenirs of Troy and nothing was left behind.

The temple of Athena was built on the northeast part of the Hisarlık mound. This temple was a huge building with thick marble columns. From this doric temple only a few marble capitals, a few marble blocks from its ceiling and a piece of the stone pavement from its terrace can be seen today. The eastern part of the two parallel temenos walls which surrounded the terrace are still standing. Some of the marble pieces from the temple were burned by local villagers to produce lime and some of them were possibly used as grave stones. For example, in Kum köy graveyard down on the plain, near the point where the River Simois joins the Scamander, and in a graveyard near Çıplak village. Also it is possible that the material in the graveyard of Eski Kumkale, an old Ottoman harbour at the mouth of the Scamander, was taken from the same source.

Down the northeast slope of the mound lies the large theatre. The stage was excavated previously and new excavations are being carried out every year. The seating capacity was probably six or eight thousand.

Partly because a greater part is unexcavated and partly because of not having many written records from this era, we do not know much about this settlement. According to recent records Ilion was completely destroyed by the Roman Legate Fimbria, during the Mithridatic Wars (85 B.C.). Soon after that Emperor Sulla provided some financial relief for rebuilding the city. This was because Ilion was recognized as the mother city of the Romans. But it especially benefitted from this legendary connection during the reign of the Julio-Claudians. At this time the city experienced a second "building boom". Augustus visited Troy in 20 B.C. The Temple of Athena, bouleuterion and the big theatre were restored or rebuilt with the financial relief provided by Augustus. Because of Ilion's legendary connection with Rome its special status as a "free and federate city" was renewed periodically. Many Roman emperors visited Troy. Caracalla was one of them. Emperor Constantine the Great also visited Troy in the early fourth century A.D. He decided to built a new capital for the Roman Empire in the east, and thought of estabilishing it in Troy. But the strategic importance of Ilion in trade had completely lost its place to Byzantium. Because of this great change, he passed over Ilion and moved to Byzantium. He rebuilt the whole city and made it the capital of the Roman Empire, and the name of the city became Constantinople.

Odeon Troy IX

Senate Troy IX

After losing its importance in trade, Ilion became more and more neglected. Only some tourists were visiting the neighbouring tumuli which were identified as tombs of the Greek and Trojan heroes. Then for a few more years the Trojans offered sacrifices at the ancient altars, but with the coming of Christianity the city lost its importance completely. In the fourth century the town became the seat of a bishopric.

Although the new excavation team is getting new information about this period today still we do not know much about this settlement or what brought this era to its end. Probably a severe earthquake in the early sixth century tumbled down the city and the people left this place forever.

Though destroyed, Troy remained. Homer and Virgil have kept it alive right up to our time.

The Aqueduct

The Great Theatre Troy IX

The Roman Aqueduct in Kemerdere Village

Homer

TROY IN MYTHOLOGY

About 3200 years ago there was a city called Troy somewhere near the Dardanelles. The peace-loving but brave people of this noble city led a happy life in peace with their king, Priam. They were engaged in farming, fishing, hunting and breading animals. This 'horse tamer' people also traded with their neighbours. Through trade as well as agriculture the Trojans became rich and had a very high standard of living. The Immortals were probably jealous of their happiness and decided to make plans for the destruction of this city.

One day Queen Hecuba had a nightmare, In her dream, fire was coming out of her stomache and the smoke from this fire was covering the whole city walls. Hecuba told her dream to Priam and later to a soothsayer. The prophecy of the soothsayer was terrible. He said that Hecuba was pregnant and the baby would cause the destruction of Troy in the future. He had to be killed as soon as he was born. Believing this, after the baby was born, King Priam gave the task to one of his men of killing the baby. The man who was in charge could not kill an innocent and defenceless new-born baby and left him in a forest on Mount Ida. He thought the wild animals would find and kill him. But a shepherd found the baby before the wild animals. This baby grew up on Mount Ida as a shepherd, and became a very handsome young man. He was the Paris who would cause problems for Troy in the future.

Paris lived on Mount Ida with a lovely nymph named Oenone, without knowing that he was a Trojan prince.

One day an interesting dispute took place on Mount Olympus. The evil goddess of discord, Eris, was not invited to a banquet at an important marriage, that of King Peleus and the sea nymph Thetis. Resenting this deeply, Eris determined to make trouble. She threw into the banqueting hall a golden apple marked "For the Fairest". Of course, all the goddesses wanted it. After long discussions, only the three great goddesses, Hera, Pallas Athena and Aphrodite remained. They went to Zeus and asked him to judge between them. But very wisely he said he would have nothing to do with the matter, because he did not want to make any of them angry. He told them to go to Mount Ida and find Paris, a royal prince who was working there as a shepherd and was an excellent judge of beauty.

This was a sort of tactic to get rid of the trouble from Mount Olympus! Obeying what Zeus said, the three goddesses came to Mount Ida with the guidance of Hermes. When they arrived at the peak, Paris was grazing his sheep down in the slopes. Hermes told him the situation and handed him the golden apple, to be given to the most beautiful goddess. When the three beautiful goddesses appeared before Paris, he realised that this would not be an easy task, for each was much more beautiful than the other. Seeing his amazement the three great goddesses offered him bribes. Hera promised to make him king of Europe and Asia. He would be the most powerful king in the world. Athena would make him the cleverest king in the world and the Trojans under his command would lay Greece in ruins. Aphrodite would give him the fairest woman in the world.

Being a simple shepherd, Paris wanted to have the most beautiful woman and gave the golden apple to Aphrodite.

This was the beginning of the Trojan war. Because according to legend, the two angry goddesses, Hera and Athena, started making plans for the destruction of Troy.

Meanwhile Aphrodite, the goddess of love and beauty, led the young prince straight to Sparta. At that time the most beautiful woman in the world was Helen. She was married to Menelaus, the king of Sparta and the brother of Agamemnon, king of Mycenae.

Menelaus and Helen received him graciously as their guest. Menelaus, trusting Paris completely, left him in his home and went off to Crete. But when he came back home Helen had gone off with Paris to Troy. He called upon all Greece to help him rescue her. All the chieftains were eager to cross the sea and lay mighty Troy in ruins, because during the wedding of Helen and Menelaus all the Greek kings had promised to help him if Helen was ever in trouble. Agamemnon, old Nestor, Ajax and Patroclos were all ready to sail to Troy. But two of them were missing: Odysseus and Achilles.

Odysseus, who was one of the shrewdest and most sensible men in Greece, did not want to leave his home and family for the sake of a faithless woman. Therefore, when the messenger came to take him to the Greek camp, he pretended that he had gone mad. He was ploughing a field and sowing it with salt instead of seed. But the messenger was shrewd too. He seized Odysseus' little son and put him in front of the plough, Odysseus turned it and saved him, thus the messenger proved that he was just as clever. Reluctantly, Odysseus had to join the army.

Achilles knew that if he went to Troy he would die before Troy fell. Therefore, wearing women's clothes he hid among the maidens in the court of Lycomedes. The chieftains sent Odysseus to find him. He disguised himself as a pedlar and went to the court. He was selling bright ornaments such as women love and also some fine weapons. While the girls flocked around the trinkets, Achilles fingered the swords and daggers. Odysseus knew him then, and knowing his destiny, Achilles went to the Greek camp with

Odysseus.

The Greek army was ready now, but this time the strong north wind was making it impossible to sail for Troy. It kept on blowing day after day. The army was desperate. At last one of the soothsayers declared that Artemis was angry because the Greeks had slain one of her beloved wild hares or deer. The only way to calm the wind was to sacrifice Ipheginia, the daughter of Agamemnon. This was hardly bearable for Agamemnon. However to help the war effort Agamemnon approved the deed. According to another legend Artemis sent a deer to be sacrificed and instead of Ipheginia the deer was sacrificed. In any case Artemis accepted the offer. The north wind ceased to blow and over a thousand ships carried more than a hundred thousand Greek fighting men to Troy.

They camped on the beach at the mouth of the Simois and the Scamander. The Greek army was very strong. They attacked Troy but Troy was well defended with very stout walls and also King Priam had many brave sons to lead the attack and to defend the holy city. Hector, the

The Beauty Contest

43

"tamer of horses", was the bravest and he was the head commander of the Trojan army. Not only this, the other Anatolian peoples accepted the Achaens as common enemies and took part on the Trojan side. The war lasted ten years. For nine years the tide of fortune swayed back and forth but neither side could gain any decided advantage. The Greeks were plundering the neighbouring settlements. In one of the plunderings Agamemnon got the daughter of Chryseis, Apollo's priest, as a prize of honour. The priest came to beg for his daughter's release. The troops wished to see the priest respected, but this was not at all to Agamemnon's liking. He refused to release the girl and rudely dismissed her father.

*"Old man, do not let me catch you loitering by the hollow ships today, nor coming back again, or you may find the god's staff and chaplet a very poor defence. Far from agreeing to set your daughter free, I intend her to grow old in Ar-*gos, *in my house, a long way from her own country, working at the loom and sharing my bed. Off with you now, and do not provoke me if you want to save your skin."*

(Iliad I. 25 - 32)

The insulted priest prayed to Apollo to send pestilence upon the Greek army. The mighty god heard him and shot fiery arrows down upon them. Many Greek soldiers sickened and died. At last Achilles called an assembly of the chieftains. He told them to either find a way to appease Apollo ar sail back home. Then the prophet Calchas said he knew why the god was angry, but that he was afraid to speak unless Achilles would guarantee his safety. Achilles agreed to this and Calchas declared that the daughter of Apollo's priest must be given back to her father.

"The god is angry because Agamemnon insulted his priest, refusing to take the ransom and free his daughter. That is the reason for our present sufferings and for those to come"

(Iliad I. 90-96)

This made Agamemnon very angry. He had no choice but to send the girl to her father. He swore at Calchas and Achilles:

"Prophet of evil, never yet have you said a word to my advantage. It is always trouble that you revel in foretelling. Not once have you fulfilled a prophecy of something good-you have never made one !"

Iliad I. 105 - 110

....
....

"But mark my words. In the same way as Phoebus Apollo is robbing me of Chryseis, whom I propose to send off in my ship with my own crew, I am going to pay a visit to your hut and take away the beautiful Briseis, your prize, Achilles, to let you know that I am more powerful than you, and to teach others not to bandy

Abduction of The Beautiful Helen

Menelaus Against Paris

words with me and openly defy their king."

Iliad I. 183-187

While he was returning the girl, he sent two of his soldiers to Achilles' tent to take his prize of honour away from him. Achilles let them take the girl without fear but he swore before gods and men that Agamemnon would pay dearly for the deed.
The sea nymph Thetis, Achilles' mother, was as angry as her son. She told Achilles to have nothing more to do with the Greeks. Going to Olympus she asked Zeus to give victory to the Trojans.

"Father Zeus, if ever I have served you well among the gods, by word or deed, grant me a wish and show your favour to my son. He is already singled out for early death, and now Agamemnon, king of men, has affronted him. He has stolen his prize and kept her for himself. Avenge my son, Olympian judge, and let the Trojans have the upper hand till the Achaeans pay him due

respect and make him full amends."

Iliad I. 503-501

The war by now reached Olympus. Some of the gods were supporting the Trojans and some of them took part on the Greek side. Aphrodite, of course was on the side of Paris. Equally, of course Hera and Athena were on the side of the Greeks. Ares, god of war, always took sides with Aphrodite. Apollo and his sister Artemis cared for Hector and for his sake helped the Trojans. Poseidon, Lord of the sea, favoured the Greeks, a sea people. Zeus liked the Trojans best, but wanted to be neutral.
While the immortals were positioning on Mount Olympus, Achilles was sitting by his ships filled with anger, neither fighting nor joining the meetings held between the Greeks. Without Achilles the Greek army was inferior to the Trojans. In spite of this the Greeks came very close to the walls of Troy. A fierce battle took place outside the walls. King Priam and the other old men watched the fight from

a tower. Suddenly the battle ceased. The armies drew back on either side. Paris, and Menelaus faced one another. The two would fight alone. If Menelaus won he would take Helen back to Sparta. If Paris won, Helen would stay in Troy. In any case the war would finish. This suggestion had come from Paris and Hector repeated Paris' suggestion to the Greek army. While the two armies were listening to Hector's speech, Helen, the cause of all the agony and death, came to the tower where King Priam and the other old Trojans were sitting and watching the battle. When they saw Helen coming to the tower, they whispered to each other:

"Who on earth could blame the Trojan and Achaean men-at-arms for suffering so long for such a woman's sake? Indeed, she is the very image of an immortal goddess. All the same, and lovely as she is, let her sail home and not stay here to vex us and our children after us."

Iliad III 154 - 160

45

Achilles And Ajax Playing A Game

Meanwhile, Priam called Helen to his side to tell him the names of the Greek heroes. and then the duel started. Paris struck first, but Menelaus caught the swift spear on his shield, then hurled his own. It rent Paris' tunic but did not wound him. Menelaus drew his sword, but it fell from his hand broken. Although unarmed he leaped upon Paris and seized him by his helmet's crest. He would have dragged him to the Greek ranks if Aphrodite had not helped Paris. She tore away the strap of the helmet and helped him escape to Troy.

Menelaus furiously went through the Trojan ranks, seeking Paris with Paris' helmet in his hand. There was nobody who would help Paris on the Trojan side, for they all hated him because he had not fought at all except to throw his spear. But he was gone, no one knew how or where. So Agamemnon spoke to both armies. He declared Menelaus the victor. As had been decided upon, the Trojans had to give Helen back. The Trojans would have agreed if Athena and Hera had not interfered. Hera was determined that the war should not end until Troy was ruined. With her prompting Athena swept down

to the battlefield and persuaded a Trojan to break the truce. Foolish Pandarus shot an arrow at Menelaus and wounded him slightly. But that was enough to start the war again. Many people were killed on both sides. The gods and goddesses were on the battlefield too. They were fighting each other.

Although the great champion, Achilles, sat alone in his tent far away from the war, the Greeks were winning. Ajax and Diomedes were fighting gloriously. Aeneas, the royal prince and son of Aphrodite, came very near to death at Diomedes' hands. Diomedes wounded him but his mother Aphrodite came to take him. Diomedes wounded Aphrodite too. It was Hera who gave him the courage to shoot at her. While Aphrodite was flying to Olympus to complain of Hera to Zeus, Apollo took Aeneas back to Troy. Remembering his promise to Thetis to avenge Achilles' wrong, Zeus ordered all the other Immortals to stay in Olympus while he himself went down to earth to help the Trojans. By now everything had changed. The Trojans had driven the Greeks back almost to their ships. That day Hector seemed irresistable "The tamer of Horses" as the Trojans called him, had never before shown himself so brilliant and so brave. The Greeks were in trouble now. Agamemnon wanted to give up and sail back to Greece, but the oldest chieftain, Nestor, told him to try to find some way of appeasing Achilles, instead of going home disgraced. Agamemnon confessed that he had acted like a fool. He begged Odysseus to go to Achilles and tell him that he was ready to give Achilles' woman back and other splendid gifts. Achilles rejected this. The next day again the Greeks were driven back. The Trojans were almost near enough to set their ships on fire. Patroclus, Achilles' best friend, saw this and begged Achilles to help the Greeks or at least to give his armour. Achilles told him he would not fight for men who had disgraced him. But he gave his armour and his men to Patroclus. Putting on the splendid armour, Patroclus led Achilles' men into battle. The Trojans thought Achilles was leading them. Indeed, for a time Patroclus fought as gloriously as Achilles, but at last he met Hector face to face and Hector's spear gave him a mortal wound. Then Hector stripped off his armour and put it on. It seemed as if he had also taken on Achilles' strength. When the bad news reached Achilles, he decided to make Hector pay with his life for the death of his best friend, Patroclus. He knew he was fated to die after Hector. He accepted this and his mother Thetis did not attempt to hold him back. She brought him new arms made by the god Hephaestus himself.

Putting the miraculous armour on, Achilles led the attack. He was fighting gloriously and seeking for Hector everywhere. The Trojans were fighting as brave man fight before the walls of their homes, under Hector's command. The gods by now were fighting as hotly as the mortals. Even the great river of Troy, Scamander, took part and strove to drown Achilles as he crossed its waters. But nothing helped. Everything was decided by the gods. Apollo knew it was of no use now to fight for Hector. The Trojans had been driven back. They opened the gates wide and took the fighting men into the city. Only Hector stood immoveable before the wall. His father Priam and his mother Hecuba cried to him to come within and save himself, but he did not heed. He thought the Trojans' defeat was his fault because he was leading them. Then Achilles came. Beside him was Athena, but Hector was alone. Apollo had left him to his fate. When Achilles and Athena came nearer, Hector turned and fled. After running three times around the walls of Troy he stopped. It was Athena who made him stop. She appeared beside him in the shape of his brother Deiphobus. That gave him courage to face Achilles. Hector cried out to Achilles:

"My lord Achilles, I have been chased by you three times round the great city of Priam without daring to stop and let you come near. But now I am going to run away no longer. I have made up my mind to fight you man to man and kill you or be killed. But first let us make a bargain, you with your gods for witness, I with mine - no compact could have better

Achilles - Hector Fight

guarantors. If Zeus allows me to endure, and I kill you, I undertake to do no outrage to your body that custom does not sanction. All I shall do, Achilles, is to strip you of your splendid armour. Then I will give up your corpse to the Achaeans. Will you do the same for me?

Achilles of the nimble feet looked at him grimly and replied: 'Hector, you must be mad to talk to me about a pact. Lions do not come to terms with men, nor does the wolf see eye to eye with the lamb- they are enemies to the end. It is the same with you and me.

(Iliad XXII. 250- 265)

So saying Achilles hurled his spear. It missed its aim, but Athena brought it back. Then Hector struck with a true aim; The spear hit the centre of Achilles' shield, but the armour was magical and could not be pierced. He turned quickly to Deiphobus to get his brother's spear, but he was not there.

Then Hector knew that Athena had tricked him. There was no way of escape, He drew his sword and attacked Achilles. Before he could approach, Achilles struck his throat with his long spear, Hector fell down. With his last breath he begged Achilles to give his body to his family. But Achilles scowled at Hector and said:

"You cur, don't talk to me of knees or name my parents in your prayers. I only wish that I could summon up the appetite to carve and eat you raw myself, for what you have done to me. But this at least is certain, that nobody is going to keep the dogs from you, not even if the Trojans bring here and weigh out a ransom ten or twenty times your worth, and promise more besides; not if Dardanian Priam tells them to pay your weight in gold- not even so shall your lady mother lay you on a bier to mourn the son she bore, but the dogs and birds of prey shall eat you up."

Iliad XXII. 345-355

So saying Achilles stripped the bloody armour from the corpse and fastened Hector's feet with thongs to the back of his chariot, letting the head trail. He dragged the dead body round the walls of Troy several times, till his fierce soul was satisfied. Patroclus' revenge was taken but his corpse had not been cremated yet. In a short time wood was cut and piled up. Patroclus' corpse was placed on top of the pile. Animals were sacrificed and the bodies were arranged in rows around the corpse. Achilles cut a handful of his own hair and threw it on the corpse as many Achaeans did. Last of all he killed a dozen brave men, the sons of noble Trojans, with his spear and added them to the pile. As he set the heap on fire he started mourning.

" All hail from me, Patroclus, in the very Halls of Hades! I am keeping all the promises I made you. Twelve gallant Trojans, sons of noble men, will be consumed by the same fire as you. For Hector son of Priam I have other plans- I will not

Achilles Dragging Dead Hector

Priam Begging Achilles

give him to the flames, I will throw him to the dogs to eat."

Iliad XXIII. 180-184

But the dogs could not aproach Hector's corpse for Aphrodite was on guard. The abuse of the dead Hector displeased all the gods except Hera, Athena and Poseidon. It especially displeased Zeus. Zeus gave Priam courage to go to Achilles, with splendid treasure. The old king went to the Greek camp and found Achilles. Priam clasped his knees and kissed his hands and begged him to give him his son's dead body. Remembering his own father he took pity on the old king and accepted the rich ransom. He gave Hector's body to his father and granted the Trojans nine days truce for the funeral. During the funeral he would keep the Greeks from fighting.

For nine days the Trojans mourned Hector. Then they cremated him and put the ashes in a golden urn and set it in a grave. They put big stones on the grave and covered it with earth thus forming a big tumulus.

After the nine days truce the fighting started again. The Ethiopian Prince Memnon came with a large army to help the Trojans. With reinforcements, even without Hector, the Trojans pressed the Greeks hard and they lost many fighting men. Finally, Achilles killed Memnon. This was his last fight. He had driven the Trojans before him up to the walls of Troy. There Paris shot a poisoned arrow at him and struck him in the heel, the only spot where he could be wounded because when Achilles was born, Thetis had made him invulnerable by dipping him into the river Styx, but the water had not covered the foot by which she was holding him. Achilles died and Ajax carried his body off the battlefield. After the funeral his ashes, together with those of Patroclus, were put in the same urn and then placed in a grave.

After Achilles' death, his splendid armour was indirectly to be the cause of the death of Ajax. A secret vote was taken amongst the Greek chieftains to decide whether Odysseus or Ajax should inherit the armour and Odysseus won. Seeing himself disgraced, Ajax commited suicide with his sword.

The death of both heroes following so closely upon each other dismayed the Greeks. Victory seemed very far away but they would not give up. Neoptolemus, the young son of Achilles, killed Paris. His death was not a great loss. Being the cause of all their sufferings, nobody was really sorry because of his death. Once his brother Hector had scolded him as follows:

"Paris, you pretty boy, you woman-struck seducer; why were you ever born? Why were not you killed before your wedding day? Yes, I could wish it so. Far better that than to be a disgrace to the rest of us, as you are, and an object of contempt. How the long - haired Achaeans must laugh when they see us make a champion of a prince because of his good looks, forgetting that he has no strength of mind, no courage, and carried off a beautiful woman from a distant land and warlike family, to be a curse to your father, to the city and to the whole people."

Iliad III. 39-50

After the death of Paris the Trojans were as strong as before and the walls stood intact. They had never really been threatened, for the greater part of the fighting had taken place at a distance from the walls.

Almost ten years had passed and the Greeks still could not get a decided advantage. To put an end to the endless war, they determined to get their army into the city and take the Trojans by suprise. But how?

Odysseus, the shrewdest of all Greeks, came up with the idea of making a wooden horse; a huge one which was hollow and big enough to hold a number of men. Odysseus and some other chieftains would hide in the horse whilst all the other Greeks would put out to sea, and hide beyond the island of Tenedos, where they could not be seen by the Trojans. If anything went wrong they would sail home. In that case, the men inside the wooden horse

Ajax Carrying The Body of Achilles

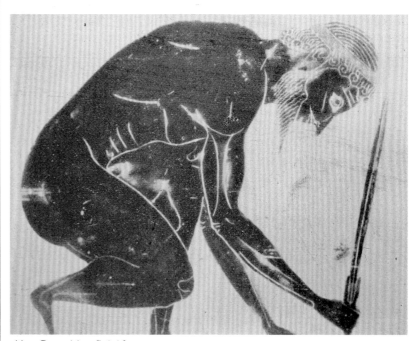

Ajax Commiting Suicide

would surely die, but if everything went as Odysseus had planned, they would sail back to Troy and wait for the signal to advance into the city. To carry out the plan they would leave behind one Greek soldier in the deserted camp, to persuade the Trojans to draw the horse into the city.

Indeed, everything went as Odysseus had planned:

One morning the Trojans awoke with astonishment. Everywhere was quiet. The noisy Greek camp was empty and the ships were gone. In front of the western gate stood a huge figure of

a horse, such as no one had ever seen. It seemed the Greeks had given up. They had accepted defeat and sailed for Greece. But what was this monstrosity for?

While they were asking eachother these questions, Sinon, the Greek who had been left behind, appeared. The Trojans seized him and dragged him before Priam. He was weeping and protesting that he no longer wished to be a Greek. Sinon told Priam that the Greeks had sacrificed Ipheginia to calm the north wind in order to be able to set sail for Troy. For their return to Greece he had been chosen to be the wretched victim to be sacrificed. They were to kill him just before their departure. All was ready, but in the night he had managed to escape and had hidden in a swamp and watched the ships sail away. It was a good story and the Trojans believed it. He went on to relate the second part of his story.

"The wooden horse" he said "had been made, as a votive offering to Athena and the reason for its huge size was to discourage the Trojans from taking it into the city. If the Trojans destroyed the horse, they would draw down Athena's anger upon them. If they brought it into the city, she would direct her favours towards the Trojans and away from the Greeks.

The story was very clever. Everybody believed it except the priest Laocoön. He said:

'Beware of the Greeks when they bear gifts'

So saying, he urged the Trojans to destroy it, but no one believed him. To prevent Laocoön from making further efforts to persuade other Trojans, Poseidon sent two fearsome serpents from the sea. They killed Laocoön and his two sons, the only doubters, and disappeared within Athena's temple.

Cassandra, the sister of Hector was another doubter. Apollo, the sun god had loved Cassandra and that was why he gave her the ability of seeing the future and she became a soothsayer. But Cassandra had refused Apollo's love so he took half of her abilities back. So she would go on seeing the future but nobody would believe her. Although she warned the Trojans about the soldiers inside the horse nobody believed her. Without hesitation the Trojans tore down the narrow western gate and through the enlarged gap dragged the horse into the city. They then refilled the gap with unworked stones. Believing the war to be over, they returned to their homes in peace as they had not done for ten years.

In the middle of the night Odysseus and his companions let themselves out of the horse one by one. Killing the guards, they opened the gates of Troy wide and marched the Greek army silently into the sleeping city. Fires were started in buildings throughout the city. The Trojans woke up and rushed out into the streets to put out the fires, but they were cut down before they realised what was happening. This was not fighting but butchery. In some parts of the town the Trojans were able to form small groups. They fought desperately to kill as many Greeks as possible before their own certain death. Some of them tore off their own armour and put on that of the dead Greeks. In this disguise they killed many Greeks, but because too many Trojans had been killed in the first onslaught, the contest was not equal. By now the end was near. Achilles' son killed old Priam in front of his wife and daughters. Before morning all the leaders were dead, except Aeneas, who with Aphrodite's help escaped from Troy with his father Ankhises and his little

Ajax Raping Cassandra at The Image of Athena. Aeneas Carrying Anchises.

Laocoön

son Ascanius. After many adventures he reached Italy. There he married the daughter of a powerful king and founded a city. Because Romulus and Remus, the actual founders of Rome, were born in this city and they were the descendents of Aeneas' family, Aeneas was always held to be the real founder of Rome.

That night Aphrodite helped Helen too. She got her out of the burning city and took her to Menelaus. He received her gladly and when he sailed for Greece she was with him.

Next morning the Greeks set sail for home. All they left behind of the proudest city of Asia was a smouldering ruin.

The Death of Priam

Neoptolemus Killing Priam, Menelaus Meeting Helen

HISTORICAL FACTS AND NEW DEVELOPMENTS

Troy occupied man's thoughts for centuries. Many artists, sculptors and painters were inspired by its legend. Tragedies and novels were written and Troy went on living in man's mind for thousand of years. And today scientists are still discussing the historical facts. New excavations are being carried on, symposiums are held and Troy is still a place of great interest.

I have been working in this most fascinating place as an official guide since 1978. I consider myself very lucky, because I have the chance of meeting many Troy enthusiasts and discussing Troy with them. My luck is still holding because I am able to follow new developments with the current excavation team. Speaking about Troy, and discussing it has become part of my daily life. To draw the reader into this interesting and most pleasant argument I have tried to find answers to the questions which were asked me by researchers, visitors and on TV programs in which I participated.

The most asked question is:

Could this small fortress really be the city of Priam which resisted the powerful Achaean army for ten years?

N.P. Skött Jörgensen, a Danish historian who used to come to the Troad almost every year in the 1980's, claims that the Troy of Priam is not at Hisarlık Hill. By changing the names of the rivers and some other places, this researcher says that 'the actual city of Priam is in "BALLIDAĞ" near Pınarbaşı. The Romans, he adds thought that Hisarlık was the ruins of the city of Priam. This is why they built Novum Ilium on Hisarlık by mistake! With this the Troy argument gained new dimensions. This Danish historian is searching for a new place for Troy at least in the Troad. A Mexican writer who put Troy somewhere in Yugoslavia succeeded in creating much excitement, especially in Yugoslavia. Yugoslavs organised a study tour to Troy. When I was guiding them in Troy they especially wanted to know the location of rivers, mountains and the islands which were mentioned in the Iliad.

After pointing out all the places, the leader of the study team looked a bit sad and disappointed, just like waking up from a beautiful dream, as if he wished the Mexican writer's claims were true. But why are these people searching for a new place for Troy?

It is true that after reading the Iliad one dreams to see remains of a glorious city. Even some romantic visitors ask where the "majestic palace of Priam" is. This "glorious city" image was certainly created by Homer, but just because we do not see ruins of a glorious city, can we still say that this was not the city of Priam?

We believe that stories told in the Iliad and other myths were not untrue but that Homer and other poets used poetic licence to exaggerate aspects of their epic poems in order to praise the Greeks. They also incorporated imaginative elements.

In light of this fact, if one knows the geography of the Troad, the ancient history and the Iliad, one can feel the vibrations of those days and feel the excitement of the Trojan war on this hill even today. Being someone who grazed sheep on the Trojan plain like Paris did on Mount Ida thousands of years ago and rode horses like Hector, I know the area very well. Everytime I read the Iliad I placed both armies somewhere on the plain and they fitted in well. I also put the Achaean fleet somewhere by the Aegean coast or a sandy beach at the beginning of the Dardanelles, it also fitted in well

Achilles Killing Penthesileia, The Queen of Amazons

with the Iliad. I sometimes searched for the wall which was built by the Greeks to protect the fleet against the Trojans. Standing at the confluence of the Scamander and the Simois I dreamed of the Trojan War and looked for the Immortals who also took part in the war. I saw owls but they did not look like the goddess Athena! The eagles, stealing the hens of the villagers, did not look like Zeus to me either! Furthermore somebody like Aphrodite never came round!

An Australian tourist who I guided through the Gallipoli war areas told me that one of his relatives who fought at Gallipoli during the First World War saw angels flying around. This story seemed to me the only way to explain the position of the Immortals.

If an Australian soldier who came from the other end of the world and fought here hopelessly and without knowing what he was fighting for saw angels flying around the Gallipoli Peninsula, 3000 years ago, almost in the same area, just on the oposite side of the Dardanelles a Greek warrior would easily see an owl as goddess Athena or he would accept an eagle as the god Zeus.

Approaching the subject with this tolerance we accept the Trojan war as an historical fact and Hisarlık hill as the city of Priam. But probably the argument should be based on whether the war took place because of kidnapping the beautiful Helen or because of economical reasons. Did the war actually last for ten years?

Modern scholars accept that the war between the Trojans and the Greeks was an actual historical fact. Of course the main reason for this long-lasting war can not have been the abduction of a beautiful woman. The main reason must have been economic, as it usually is.

We know that the Greeks started establishing trade colonies on the Black sea coast much before the Trojan war. From this point of view the Dardanelles were indispensible to the seafaring and trading Greeks. Which helped Troy become an important trading centre and the Trojans middlemen or possibly the Greeks had to pay very high taxes to go through the Dardanelles. That could have been the reason King Priam became very wealthy. To put an end to this inconvenience, the Greeks may have acted together, using the abduction of the beautiful Helen as a pretext.

The Greeks' coming to Anatolia did not look like one of the migrations which Anatolia had so often. It was the first time a different nation from another continent had attacked Anatolia. Cities were burned and plundered. Women were kidnapped. Here was a common enemy for all Anatolia. This is why all the Anatolian people took part on the Trojan side. Even the Amazons, legendary women soldiers, were allies of the Trojans. This was in a way a fight between Asia and Europe and probably lasted more than ten years. The Dorians who came to Greece from the north were pressing the Achaeans. The Achaeans needed new lands and Anatolia attracted them. The Greek troops kept on coming to Anatolia for many years. Anatolians resisted them everywhere. Probably the longest resistance took place in Troy and several epics telling of events which took place at different parts of Anatolia could well have been put together by poets as if they all took place at Troy. As a matter of fact the Iliad mentions the plundering of cities. On the other hand, the founders of many Ionion cities were the descendents of the Greek heroes who had joined in the Trojan war. In addition to that, no city could resist being besieged for ten years nor could the surrounding invaders endure for so long.

The Building Material of Senato

LAW OF THE BYZANTINE EMPEROR ANASTASIUS I. (491-518 AD)
REGULATING PASSAGE THROUGH THE DARDANELLES
Archaeological Museum - ISTANBUL

Whoever dares to violate these regulations, shall be punished. Besides, the administrator of the Dardanelles must have the right of receiving 50 golden Litrons. So secret or evil activity, and be always alert, efficient and hard-working. We have decreed that our orders be engraved on stone plaques and that these be erected as near as possible to the sea shore so that all men who want to may see them and all the other men we want to see them can see them. These plaques must be erected in this area, just in front. On one hand those who display courage in order not to be punished must equally be able to read them. The distinguished governor and mayor of the capital, who already has both hands full of things to do, has turned to our lofty piety in order to reorganize the entry and exit of all ships through the Dardanelles, and change the rules which have been obeyed by sailors for the last 22 years.

Starting from our day and also in the future, anybody who wants to pass through the Dardanelles must pay the following:
- All wine merchants who bring wine to the capital (Constantinopolis) except Cilicians, have to pay the Dardanelles officials 6 follis and 2 sextarius of wine.
- In the same manner, all merchants of olive oil, vegetables and lard must pay the Dardanelles officials 6 follis, Cilician sea merchants have to pay 3 follis and in addition to that I keration to enter, and 2 keration to exit.
- All wheat merchants have to pay the officials 3 follis per madius: 4-6 kg when entering the Dardanelles, and a further sum of 3 follis when leaving.

WHO WERE THE TROJANS?

Because the Iliad was written in Ancient Greek and all the names of the persons and gods were Greek names, many people think that the Trojans and the Greeks were the same people and they spoke the same language. The abundance of the Mycenaean type of ceramics which were found during the excavations also strengthens this opinion. But according to the latest research of linguists, the Trojans spoke an Indo-European language which was widely spoken in different part of Anatolia, called Luvian.

Prof. Calvert Watkins, a specialist in Indo-European languages, explains the abundance of Mycenaean ceramics as due to trade and claims that during this trade two different languages were used. It is clearly understood from the Iliad that the Trojans had a close relationship with the Greeks. Equally they had similar relationships with the Hittites as well. As a matter of fact there is a resemblance between the marriage traditions of the Trojans and the Hittites. For example: According to a Hittite law " if a man has a wife and the man dies, his brother takes his wife". The Trojans had exactly the same law. The legend tells us that after the death of Paris his brother Deiphobos married Helen.

Obviously the Trojans had connections both with east and west. But who were they? It would probably be easier to answer this question if a few written tablets had been unearthed during the excavations. But no tablets have been found so far. However the Hittites in central Anatolia used both Hierogliphics and Cuneiform, around the second millennium B.C. This is why the linguists are searching the Hittite sources and trying to find something about Troy.

At a Symposium held at Bryn Mawr College in October 1984 linguist Prof. Watkins suggests that "Steep Wilusa", a city mentioned on a Hittite tablet which was written in Luvian, could well be "Steep Ilios" of the Iliad. "Priya-Muwas" sounds very much like "Priamos". The Luvian "Alaksandus" may well be "Aleksandros", the second name of the Trojan prince Paris.

How can we ignore these resemblances? Especially if Homer tells us in the Iliad that the Trojans and their allies spoke different languages and dialects.

"Hector, I urge you above all to do as I say. In his great city, Priam has many allies. But these foreigners all talk different languages. Let their own captains in each case take charge of them, draw up their countrymen, and lead them into battle.

Iliad II. 800-805

"

..Such was the babel that went up from the great Trojan army, which hailed from many parts, and being without a common language used many different cries and calls.

Iliad IV. 437-439

That means the Trojans and their allies were certainly not Greek-speaking people. The names of many heroes mentioned in the Iliad were local Anatolian names. Those which sound Greek were either adopted or made up. For example "Astyanax", son of Hector, was a Greek name, but Hector would call him "Skamandrias". "Hector" too could well have born a real local Anatolian name

Although not proved, we shall go on believing that the Trojans were "native people of Anatolia" until archaeologists find tablets in future proving to the contrary.

Houses of Troy VI And VII

WHY HISARLIK ?

Many visitors wonder why Hisarlık Hill was chosen by the Trojans to build their city.

First of all, prehistoric men always preferred to built settlements on hill tops. It is obvious that ease of defence is the main reason for this. Not only this, there are other factors for Hisarlık for being chosen as a place for building a city. For example, Hisarlık is a hill dominating a fertile plain. Besides farming and animal breeding, it was a very convenient place for hunting. The swamp down on the plain was a heaven for hunters till the swamp was drained, only half a century ago.

On the other hand the topography of Troy was very different from today. "Paleo - geography", the geography of the past, is a new science which is widely used today in archaeology. It is sort of mixture of geology and geography, in other words the knowledge which is gained through geological researches is applied to geography. As a result of paleogeographic studies it is possible to make maps of river deltas or sea shores as they were centuries ago. Historical events or ancient civilisations are interpreted once again with the help of these maps.

John C. Kraft, head of the Geology department of Delaware University and Prof. Ilhan Kayan and Oğuz Erol from Ankara University made some paleogeographic studies around Troy. According to these scientists, 5000 years ago, that is, during

A View of The Plain of Troy

Troy I. the sea came up to Troy, but later the two rivers silted up the plain. This shallow sea port at the entrance to the Dardanelles was therefore at that time an ideal place for fishing.

All these factors explain why this spot was chosen. As well as this, settlements in Anatolia first began being fortified after 3000 B.C. Troy I was one of the first cities in Anatolia to be fortified. This is another indication of the importance of Hisarlık hill. Later, with the development of international trade, the importance of Troy at the mouth of the Dardanelles increased. Because of its strategic position on this waterway it was occupied for more than 3500 years and destroyed and rebuilt nine times.

SEA SHELLS

Sea shells everywhere in the ruins attract almost every visitor's attention. They ask why there are so many. We sometimes wondered whether they ate them because we saw some together with animal bones. We discussed this possibility with some archaeologists in the excavation team. They found this possibility acceptable but we have observed sea shells in mudbricks solidified as a result of fire. That makes us think there is another possibility:

We know that the best material for mudbrick is the soil of the plain. As we have mentioned before the plain of Troy was once under water, this is why the soil contained sea shells. These sundried bricks with sea shells in

them became soil after earthquakes destroyed the mudbrick houses and the shells were scattered around.

Sea Shells

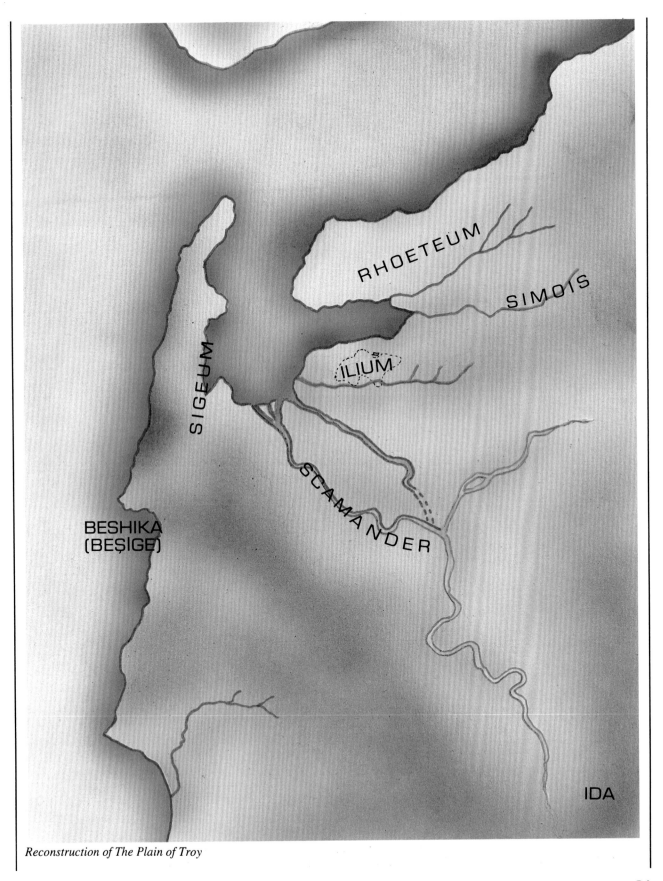

RHOETEUM

SIMOIS

ILIUM

SIGEUM

SCAMANDER

BESHIKA
(BEŞİGE)

IDA

Reconstruction of The Plain of Troy

THE POPULATION OF TROY

After having a general idea about the size of Troy, a question about the population of this small fortified settlement comes to mind. What was the population of Troy during the Trojan War? The Iliad is the only source to find an answer for this question:

In Book II of the Iliad, the verses between 510 and 750 tell us the names of the Greek chieftains and the number of their ships. In total we find 1200. Each of the ships could carry 120 warriors. That means according to the Iliad roughly 144000 Greek warriors came to Troy. Again in the second book we read as follows:

....

"..if we and the Trojans made a truce and each side held a count, the enemy reckoning only native Trojans and we Achaeans numbering off in tens, with the idea that each of our squads should have a Trojan to pour out its wine, many a squad would go without a steward.

....

Unfortunately, they have numerous and well-equipped allies from many towns, who thwart me and defeat all efforts to bring down the great stronghold of Ilium."
Iliad II. 125 - 134

That means the Trojans were less than one tenth of the Greeks in number. So the Trojans had an army of ten to fifteen thousand warriors. This can not be reliable because of the poetic exaggeration of the epics. Instead of making estimations about the population of Troy from those numbers, it is better to turn to the question of how many people could shelter in the fortress.

First of all this small settlement was an acropolis. In other words, it was a fortress which surrounded the temples, state buildings and palaces. That means the fortress was only for the king and his family and some other state dignitaries. Ordinary people lived outside the city walls in the lower city which is still unexcavated. To say " 500 or 1000 people lived in the fortress" would not be the answer which the visitor would like to hear. Probably the most logical answer is that the Trojans, together with their Anatolian allies, resisted the Greeks with a force equal in number.

HOW DID THE TROJANS OBTAIN WATER?

During peacetime the Trojans gathered water from the fresh water streams or from the rivers. A cave in the unexcavated lower city can still be seen today. No doubt once a fresh water stream came out of this cave and joined the Scamander. Besides this smaller springs existed until recently. On one of these streams a fountain was built by the author's father in 1953 which was called" the fortress fountain" by the local people. As time passed all the small streams including the fountain dried up.

During peace time the Trojans did not have a water problem, but for emergencies they built wells and cisterns inside the defence system. The well-cistern inside the northern tower is the biggest of all. The water problem of the Roman city was solved by terracotta pipe lines and aqueducts. The acquaduct in Kemerdere village is a part of the water system which supplied water for New Ilion.

THE TREASURE OF PRIAM

"The gold of Troy" found by Schliemann became the subject of novels and many visitors are very much interested in the treasure. Schliemann made many mistakes which can not be tolerated with our present understanding of archaeology. He turned Troy into a molehill. In spite of this he was considered the Father of Archaeology and he was even awarded a Ph.D. in archaeology. He is described by some writers as "the most unscientific of archaeologists who founded the science of archaeology". He imagined King Priam as a rich king which is why when he found treasure in Troy he called it the "treasure

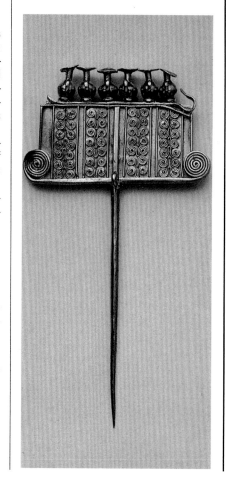

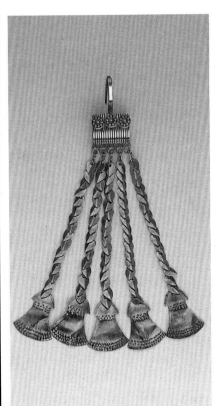

Some Immitations of The Treasure

of Priam", because he had the habit of giving heroic names to his discoveries. He believed that they were the jewels of Helen. Putting them on his wife Sophia, he addressed her "you are my beautiful Helen", but we know today that the treasure was at least 1000 years earlier than the time of Priam, belonging to the second settlement at Hisarlık.

The only explanation for not finding any trace of the real treasure of Priam must be the plundering of the whole city at the end of the Trojan War. "The treasure of Troy" was smuggled by Schliemann to Greece then later taken to Berlin. It was kept in a museum until the Second World War then disappeared.

According to some sources, during the Second World War the museum was plundered by Nazi officers. If this is true it is now in private hands in Latin America.

According to other sources the Russians who first entered Berlin first plundered the museum and transported it to Russia.

Because this last one seemed more probable to us, we mentioned this possibility to a Russian ambassador whom I guided around Troy. The only answer we got from the ambassador was "nyet" in Russian which means "no".

With no further comment this short answer was suspicious. Then we read in the newspapers that it is in Pushkin Museum in Moscow. This has been confirmed by the Russian government. Part of the treasure which was given back by Schliemann to the Ottoman government as a gesture to get the second permission for excavations and part of that which was found during later excavations, is now on display in the Archaeological Museum in Istanbul.

We hope one day all the artifacts including the treasure, will be returned to where they belong and exhibited in a museum together with that recently found.

Beşik Hill And The Island of Tenedos

BEŞIK BAY OR HELLESPONT?

Even after Schliemann's dream had come true and the prehistoric settlement at Hisarlık was accepted as the city of Priam by scientists the discussions about Troy did not come to an end. One of the subjects discussed at a symposium held in Bryn Mawr college in October 1984 was the location of the Greek camp and the ships.

"Fill him with desperate courage until such time as the Achaeans shall reach the ships and HELLESPONT in rout."

Iliad XV 231-233

"While she was on her journey to Olympus, the Achaean men-at-arms, fleeing with cries of terror from men-killing Hector, reached the ships and the HELLESPONT"

Iliad XVIII. 150-151

As we understand from these lines, according to the Iliad the Greeks landed at the mouth of the Scamander river on the Hellespont. But some scientists do not agree with this. One of them is Prof. Manfred Korfmann who directed the excavations in Beşik bay and is still directing the excavations in Troy. By taking account of some important factors like, "the water sources", "the strong and nearly ceaseless winds which usually blow from the northeast" and "the current of the Dardanelles", Korfmann claims that Beşik Bay is the only convenient place for anchorage and embarkation.

First of all, on the slopes around Beşik bay there are enough fresh water sources to cover the needs of a big army even for a long time. Also, the sea in Beşik Bay is shallow and sandy. The seafarers of prehistoric times could easily beach their ships along the sandy shores. Besides this, according to paleo-geographic soundings the basin has silted up following the erosion of the surrounding hills. So the bay extended far inland thus offering an even more protective harbour than today. But the current in the Dardanelles is very strong, especially in spring time with the melting snow and rain when the rivers which flow into the Black Sea carry far more fresh water. The current runs through the Dardanelles at a speed of 9km. per hour. By adding to this the negative effect of the north wind with an average speed of 16 km. per hour, it can be understood that during the Trojan War when the technique of sailing against the wind had not been discovered, the mouth of Scamander, which is open to the north wind, would not be a convenient place for anchorage and embarkation.

During the excavations near Beşik Bay, remains of a port were unearthed. In particular graves were uncovered a few metres from the ancient sea shore from the 13 th. century B.C. Those graves could well be the graves of the Achaeans who camped here. In addition paleo-geographic studies show that the topography of the plain of Troy was very different from the present. For example, around 2000 B.C. the sea level was 1m. higher than today. These scientists believe that "the axis of the battlefield lay to the south of Troy and to the east of Beşik bay. Thus they suggest that Beşik Bay should be considered the site of the Achaean camp. They also recommend the results of their studies be read by scholars of the Iliad and Odyssey to reconsider some of their interpretations in the light of the geological and geographical analyses.

Without objecting to these hypotheses, I think that some of the Achaeans who had rowing boats, despite the strong wind and current, camped on both sides of the mouth of Scamander. If the Achaeans came to Troy with 1200 ships as told in the Iliad, they might have camped at Sigeum and Rhoeteum as well as Beşik Bay. For example, I believe that Achilles, who had a quarrel with Agamemnon, camped far away from him.

Piece of A Ceiling Block at Kumköy Graveyard

NEW EXCAVATIONS

The new excavations in Troy started in 1988. Permission was given to Prof. Manfred Korfmann, a prehistorian at Tübingen University in Germany.

The excavations are carried out with modern methods and fresh knowledge of archaeology. New measurements with modern tools have already been completed. About 60 experts in different fields and from different countries have been continuing the excavations every year for three month terms in June, July and August. During the excavation season even the smallest ceramic piece is collected and studied and carbon 14 method is used for datings.

Besides stopping the deterioration of the ruins, the main aim of the new excavation is to study carefully the different strata of this most important settlement on the northeastern corner of the "Anatolian Bridge". We believe that for such work Troy was not chosen by chance.

Over the "Anatolian Bridge" so many different peoples passed either from Asia to Europe or from Europe to Asia over the centuries. These peoples from different races and different cultures left traces in Troy as they were passing by. The results of the studies of these traces will throw light on the whole history of Europe because many Eu-

ropean nations claim that they are either the descendents of the Trojans or originally came from a corner of Anatolia. For example the founders of Rome the twin brothers Romulus and Remus were the descendents of Aeneas, a Trojan prince. This is why the Romans declared themselves as grandchildren of the Trojans and Troy the mother city of Rome. French people also claim that they come from a Trojan family. We wonder if the name "Paris" was given to the capital of France by coincidence or because of the mythological connection with Troy.

The Welsh people in the west of Britain also believe that they are descendents of the Trojans. In fact the Galatians (or Gauls) were a Celtic people who lived in Asia Minor. They lived somewhere not far from Troy and were the biggest enemies of the Pergamon people. After the Pergamon army defeated them, they migrated to Europe via Yugoslavia. Their struggle with the Pergamon army is described on the reliefs of the famous Zeus Altar as the fight of giants and gods.

On the relief gods symbolise the people of Pergamon and giants symbolise the Galatians.

According to an English legend one of the followers of Aeneas was called Brutus. They left Troy together but later Brutus quarrelled with Aeneas. As Aeneas was sailing to Italy Brutus sailed to Great Britain. There he fought with giants and defeated them. Because of Brutus the island was called Britain. This is why the English, like the Romans, thought they were the descendants of the Trojans, claiming that the original name of London was "Troy Novant", the "new Troy".

The above mentioned claims may all be myths but still it shows European nations' interest in Troy seeking their roots somewhere in Anatolia. In fact, it is accepted today that the Trojans spoke "Luvian", an Indo-European language, the same as that spoken in many European countries.

Troy has remains dating from 3000 B.C. till 400 A.D. That means this place was inhabited for 3400 years or even more. During recent excavations under the ruins of Troy I. an earlier settlement was discovered which goes back till 3500 B.C. Like many visitors we call it "Troy O" but the archaeologists of the excavation team call it more scientificly, "an earlier settlement than Troy I".

If we take all these factors into account we understand better why Troy was chosen as a reference point by archaeologists. We also believe that the results from all this careful work at Troy are going to be very useful for the study of other ancient places in Anatolia.

In this international excavation team, besides German and Turkish archaeologists, American, English, Austrian and Dutch archaeologists are taking part. The excavations are carried out under the control of the Ministry of Culture. All artifacts found during the excavations are registered and stored in the Archaeological Museum in Çanakkale.

The scientific results are also published annually as reports. Mercedes Benz sponsors a great deal of the excavations.

During the 1991 excavation season many Byzantine graves were found on the site of the big theatre. Similar graves were found a few years ago everywhere in Troy. This brings to mind the question of whether there was Byzantine settlement as well... in other words was there Troy X too? This is not clear so far. Probably Troy was accepted as a holy place even during the Byzantine period. Ilion became a place of pilgrimage and some people perhaps wanted to be buried here.

THE TOMBS

On the hills which surround the plain of Troy some unusual hills attract many visitors' attention. Those hills are shown on some old maps as the graves of Achilles, Patroclus or Ajax. But it can not be proven today whether they were the graves of the Greek heroes or not. It is believed that they are from Hellenistic times but even so there might be earlier graves underneath. It is also possible that the tombs might have been built during the time of Alexander the Great symbolically in the name of these Greek heroes as grave monuments. As a matter of fact, after the Trojan War Anatolia became a Greek land. The death place of the important Greek warriors like Achilles, Patroclus and Ajax was accepted as a holy place. Troy became a place of pilgrimage, in other words a tourist centre. Alexander the Great visited the grave of Achilles, the person he admired most, and sacrificed animals there. He also ordered his generals to build a temple to Athena at Troy. He may also have ordered more soil put on the graves in order to give them a monumental appearance. If at least one of these tombs was excavated, we would be able to get a better idea what they are. On the horizon of Troy today they look very much like the memorials from the First World War on the other side of the Dardanelles.

Trace of Earth Quake

THE WOODEN HORSE

The wooden horse at the entrance of the ruins attracts many visitors attention. Although it was built in 1975 as a tourist attraction, today it has become the focus of the "wooden horse argument"

Was there ever a wooden horse?

If there was, was it as big as this one?

How many soldiers were hidden in the horse?

Did the original horse look like this one?

Is this the original horse!!?

These sort of half-serious half-joking questions are asked almost every day around the horse. Some visitors find it amusing and take a picture of it. Of course there are some visitors who do not like it at all. Whether one likes it or not it has become the symbol of Troy. Here we would like to speak about whether there was actually a wooden horse and if there was, why was it built?

The wooden horse is briefly mentioned only in the Odyssey, not in the Iliad. According to legend it was used as a war trick. That is, it was left behind as an offering to the goddess Athena by the Greeks. The Trojans took it inside the city walls without realising there were soldiers in it. In the night the Greek soldiers came out and killed the guards. The Greek army marched into the city and conquered Troy. To find a more logical explanation for the wooden horse some scholars invented better theories.

Austrian Prof. Schachermeyr and Turkish Prof. Ekrem Akurgal claim that the wooden horse was built as an offering for Poseidon, the Earthshaker and God of the Sea. According to this theory the city walls which defended Troy against the Greeks for ten years were destroyed by a violent earthquake. The Greeks attacked Troy and conquered it. Since the Greeks thought that Poseidon had helped them by destroying

Troy's defence system, they built a wooden horse as a votive offering to him.

Michael Wood, in his book "In search of the Trojan war", which was shown on BBC TV as a series, suggests that a wooden horse might have been built as a battering ram to destroy the walls. This theory was inspired by an Assyrian relief and seems logical. The Achaean soldiers tried several times to climb the sloping walls but could not climb the vertical part which was made of mudbrick. A horse - like battering ram could well have been used against this weak part of the wall.

And last of all, a wooden tank-like horse could have been used as a big shield to approach the walls, or as a moveable tower from which soldiers jumped onto the walls.

We leave the interpretation of these different hypotheses to the reader.

Assyrian Battering Ram

THE SURROUNDINGS OF TROY

In the Troad almost 90 ancient settlements have been discovered. Beside Troy, the most important ones are Assos, Alexandria-Troas, Chryse, Lampsakos, Sestos, Dardanos, Neandria, Parkote, Asisbe, Priapos, Parion, Kebrene, Skepsis, Gallipolis, Tenedos, Imbros, Abydos and Sigeon. Assos especially is attracting more and more visitors day by day. The greater part of the city walls of Assos from the Hellenistic Period are still standing.

During recent excavations in the necropolis interesting types of graves were unearthed. The work for reconstruction of the archaic Athena temple is still going on at the summit of the volcanic hill. The towers on both sides of the western gate are still in good condition. Even the gutters can be seen.

The famous Greek philosopher Aristotle lived here and gave lessons in the Assos school of philosophy.

Behramkale village was built over the ruins of Assos. Ancient stones were used to build the new houses.

Alexandria-Troas was built as a port on the orders of Alexander the Great to make a sea connection between Anatolia and Greece. Today an archway from the Roman baths can still be seen. An ancient harbour is located behind the village of Dalyan. When the early Christians started to come to Anatolia, St. Paul visited Alexandria-Troas and preached there and left Anatolia from this harbour for Greece. In the Bible there is a section about St. Paul's preachings in Alexandria-Troas.

Nowadays many biblical tours are organised to this place.

Hisarlık From An Aeroplane